J. Dennis Harris

A Summer on the Borders of the Caribbean sea

J. Dennis Harris

A Summer on the Borders of the Caribbean sea

ISBN/EAN: 9783743321830

Manufactured in Europe, USA, Canada, Australia, Japa

Cover: Foto ©ninafisch / pixelio.de

Manufactured and distributed by brebook publishing software (www.brebook.com)

J. Dennis Harris

A Summer on the Borders of the Caribbean sea

ON

THE BORDERS

OF

THE CARIBBEAN SEA.

BY J. DENNIS HARRIS.

WITH AN INTRODUCTION BY
GEORGE WILLIAM CURTIS.

NEW YORK:
A. B. BURDICK, PUBLISHER,
No. 145 NASSAU STREET.
1860.

ADVERTISEMENT.

Through the columns of leading journals in New York, St. Louis, and other localities, we have had occasion to acknowledge the fact that the political views which gave rise to the present volume, though comparatively new, have generally met the approval of distinguished statesmen and philanthropists, North and South.*

The following note from the venerable Mr. Giddings indicating the proposition, is but one of a large number which we have received from various parts of the country:—

Jefferson, Ohio, July 13, 1859.

My Dear Sir:—I am heartily in favor of Mr. Blair's plan of furnishing territory in Central America for the use of such of our African brethren as wish to settle in a climate more congenial to the colored race than any that our government possesses.

I hope and trust you may be successful in your efforts.

Very truly,

J. D. Harris, Esq.   J. R. GIDDINGS.

The subjoined, respecting the work itself, is from Mr. Wil-

---

* See Appendix.

liam Cullen Bryant, by whom, in addition to Mr. George W. Curtis, a portion of these communications was reviewed:—

Roslyn, Long Island, August 26, 1860.

Dear Sir:—I have looked over with attention the letters you left with me, and return them herewith. It appears to me it will be very well to publish them. Of the Spanish part of the island of San Domingo very little is known—much less than of the French part; and the information you give of the country and its people is valuable and interesting.

I am, Sir,

Respectfully yours,

Mr. J. D. Harris.   W. C. BRYANT.

CONTENTS.

INTRODUCTION.. vii

DOMINICAN REPUBLIC.

LETTER I.
From New York to Puerto de Plata — Smoothness of the Voyage — Hayti in the Distance — The Custom-House Officers — Description of the Standing Army — Unparalleled Scenic Beauty........ 13-19

LETTER II.
Want of Information — One side of a Question — The other side — Causes of the decline of the Spanish Colony — Subsequent history 20-30

LETTER III.
Corpus Christi — The Farm of the Fugitive Slave.................... 31-35

LETTER IV.
First Ride in the Country — Pastoriza Place........................ 36-41

LETTER V.
Valley of the Isabella — Customs of the People — A Call for Dinner.. 42-50

LETTER VI.
On the way to Porto Cabello — Antille-Americana — Immigration Ordinance.. 51-61

LETTER VII.
Proposed American Settlement — A Picture of Life — Tomb of the Wesleyan Missionary 62-67

LETTER VIII.
Summary of Dominican Staples, Exports, and Products............... 68-75

CONTENTS.

REPUBLIC OF HAYTI

HISTORICAL SKETCH.

LETTER IX.
State of Affairs previous to 1790.................................... 76–83

LETTER X.
Affairs in France — Case of the Mulattoes — Terrible Death of Ogé and Chavine 84–92

LETTER XI.
Tragedy of the Revolution — A Chapter of Horrors (which the delicate reader may, if he pleases, omit)................................. 93–104

LETTER XII.
Tragedy of the Revolution, continued — Rigaud succeeded by L'Ouverture — L'Ouverture duped by Le Clerc 105–115

LETTER XIII.
The War Renewed — "Liberty or Death" — Expulsion of the French — Jean Jacques Dessalines, First Emperor of Hayti — The Aurora of Peace — Principal Events up to present date — Geffrard on Education..116–127

GRAND TURK'S AND CAICOS ISLANDS.

LETTER XIV.
An Island of Salt — Honor to the British Queen — Sir Edward Jordan, of Jamaica — A Story in Parenthesis — The Poetry of Sailing....128–137

BRITISH HONDURAS.

LETTER XV.
Off Ruatan — The Sailor's Love Story — Sovereignty of the Bay Islands — English vs. American View of Central American Affairs........138–150

CONCLUSIVE SUMMARY.

LETTER XVI.
Concise Description of the Spanish Main — Dominicana Reviewed — The magnificent Bay of Samana — Conclusive Summary.........151–160

APPENDIX.
The Anglo-African Empire — Opinions of distinguished Statesmen and Philanthropists... 161–179

INTRODUCTION.

THE free colored American, of whatever shade, sees that his destiny is linked with slavery. Where his face is a crime he can not hope for justice. In the country which enslaves his race he can never be an acknowledged man. That it is his native country does not help him. The author of this book is an American as much as James Buchanan. He is more so: for the father of Mr. Buchanan was born in Ireland, and the father of Mr. Harris was born in North Carolina. But the one becomes president; the other is officially declared to have no rights which white men are bound to respect.

The intelligent colored man, therefore, as he ponders the unhappy condition of his race among us, perceives that, even if slavery in the Southern States were to be immediately abolished, his condition would be only nominally and legally, not actually, equal to that of the whites. The traditional habit of unquestioned mastery can not be laid aside at will. Prejudice is not amenable to law. There is a terrible logic in the slave system. For the proper and safe subjugation of the slave there must be silence, ignorance, and absolute despotism. But these react upon the master; and the difficulties and dangers of emancipation, as the history of Jamaica shows, are found upon the side of the master and not of the slave. The law might establish a political equality between them, but the old feeling would survive, and would still exclaim with the San Domingo planters when the French Assembly freed the mulattoes in 1791, "We would rather die than share our political rights with a bastard and degenerate race."

The free colored man, wishing to help himself and his race, may choose one of several methods. If he dare to take the risk, he may try to recover by force the rights of which force only deprives him. But his truest friends among the dominant race will assure him that such a course is mere suicide. In a war of races in this country his own would be exterminated. Or he may say with Geo. T. Downing, "I feel that I am working for the people with whom I am identified in oppression, in securing a business name: I shall strive for my and their elevation, but it will be by a strict and undivided attention to business." Or he may believe with Jefferson, "Nothing is more certainly written in the book of fate than that these people [the colored] are to be free: nor is it less certain that the two races equally free can not live in the same government. Nature, habit, opinion, have drawn indissoluble lines of distinction between them."

This latter opinion is shared by many intelligent public men in this country, of whom Francis P. Blair, Jr., of Missouri, Senator Doolittle, of Wisconsin, and Senator Bingham, of Michigan, are the most conspicuous. They believe that the emigration of free colored people, protected by the United States, into some region of propitious climate and beyond the taint of prejudice against color, would have the most important practical influence upon the question of emancipation in this country, and of the consequent restoration of the colored race to the respect of the world.

It is not surprising that a docile and amiable people enslaved by nearly half the States,—legally excluded from many of the rest, and everywhere contemned, should believe this, and turn their eyes elsewhere in the fond faith that any land but their own is friendly.

The author of this book is of opinion that under the protection of the United States government a few intelligent and industrious colored families could colonize some spot within the Gulf of Mexico or upon its shores, and there live usefully and respected; while gradually an accurate knowledge of the advantages of such a settlement would be spread among their friends in the United States, and, as they developed their capacities for labor and society, not only attract their free brethren to follow, but enable the well-disposed slaveholders to see an easy and simple solution of the question which so deeply perplexes them, "What should we do with the emancipated slaves?"

But neither Mr. Harris nor his friends, so far as I know, anticipate the final solution of the practical problem of slavery by emigration. They do not contemplate any vast exodus of their race; for they know how slowly even the small results they look for must be achieved, since the first condition is the protection of the American government. Mr. Harris thinks that the island of Hayti or San Domingo, in its eastern or Dominican portion, offers the most promising prospect for such an experiment; and this little book is the record of his own travel and observation upon that island and at other points of the Caribbean sea. It contains a brief and interesting sketch of the insurrection of Toussaint L'Ouverture, a story which incessantly reminds every thoughtful man that slavery everywhere, however seemingly secure, is only a suppressed, not an extinguished, volcano.

I commend the book heartily as sincere and faithful, quite sure that it will command attention not only by its intrinsic interest and merit, but as another silent and eloquent protest against the system which, while it deprives men of human rights, also denies them intellectual capacity. I think we may pardon the author that he does not love the government of his native land. But surely he and all other colored men may congratulate themselves that the party whose principles will presently control that government repeats the words of the Declaration of Independence as its creed of political philosophy.

GEORGE WILLIAM CURTIS.

New York, *September 1st*, 1860.

A SUMMER

ON THE BORDERS OF

THE CARIBBEAN SEA.

LETTER I.

Dominican Republic.

FROM NEW YORK TO PUERTO DEL PLATA — SMOOTHNESS OF THE VOYAGE — HAYTI IN THE DISTANCE — DESCRIPTION OF THE STANDING ARMY — UNPARALLELED SCENIC BEAUTY.

> "Is John departed, and is Lilburn gone?
> Farewell to both, to Lilburn and to John."
> HUDIBRAS.

IT was a mild, showery morning on the 19th of May, 1860, that the brig John Butler, on board of which we were, left her dock at New York and anchored off the Jersey Flats. From this point we enjoyed the pleasantest and decidedly most satisfactory view of the great commercial city and its environs. The many white-sailed vessels and finely-painted steamers plying in and out the North and East rivers, and between the bright green undulating slopes of Staten and Long islands, presented a picturesque and animated scene, quite in contrast with the dark walls and stately steeples of the city which arose beyond.

More delightfully refreshing nothing could have been. Altogether, the fine air and characteristic scenes of New York bay amply repaid the inconvenience of remaining all day in sight of the great metropolis, without being jostled in its streets or snuffing the peculiar atmosphere that pervades it.

On the morning of the 20th we sailed out of the bay, passed Sandy Hook, and were at sea. The sky was clear, and the ocean calm. Betwixt the novelty of being at sea for the first time and the dread of that sickness which all landsmen fear, but know to be inevitable, I was kept in a state of moderate excitement which effectually annihilated those sentimental sorrows which one is expected at such times to entertain. The first vessel we met coming in was the Porto Plata, from this city, and owned by a German firm on the corner of Broadway and Wall street, New York. Her cargo, I have since learned, consisted principally of mahogany and hides.

Our mornings were passed mostly in studying the Dominican language, which, as nearly as I can analyze it, is a compound of Spanish, French, English, Congo, and Caribbean—but, of course, principally Spanish. The afternoons were spent in fishing, and catching sea-weed, watching the flying-fish, or in looking simply and silently on the ever-bounding sea, which was in itself an infinite and unwearying source of irrepressible delight. A comparatively quiet sameness characterized the voyage. With bright clouds pencilling the sunset sky, a fresh breeze stiffening the sails, and the ship gliding smoothly over the buoyant waves, the sensations were at times exceedingly exhilarating, and even supremely delicious. But there were no dead calms, no terrific storms. To-day was the pale blue sky above, and the deep blue ocean rolling everywhere around; and to-morrow the sky was equally as fine, and the same dark heaving ocean as boundlessly sublime. Had there been a storm, if only for description's sake!

But the poetry ceased. We were now in the latitude of the regular trade-winds, with which every man is supposed to be as certainly familiar as he is with a school-book, or the way to church. Where were the winds? Wanting—from the south and east when they should have been from the west, and *vice versa*. As for their reputed regularity, they were no more regular than a sinner at prayers. Four successive days we averaged about one mile an hour, and this was in the trade-winds! For the honor of all concerned, however, I will say (on the point-blank oath of our captain) that such a thing never occurred before, and, as he expressed it, "mightn't be again in a thousand years." I thought of an old man who once went travelling, and when he returned he was asked what he had learned. He said, simply, "I was a fool before, but by travelling I found it out." The astounding thunderstorms you hear about in the West Indies were all gone before we got here; so were the whirlwinds.

After a sail of twelve days, a long, dim, bluish outline, as of a cloud four hundred miles in length, stood out above the waves. Soon, with a glass, could be distinguished the regularly rising tablelands and lovely green valleys, the dark mountains standing in the background. I was at once agitated with all the anxieties of hope and fear. We were approaching the eventful shores of San Domingo, embracing as it does the Dominican and Haytien republics. But however thrillingly interesting its past history may have been, the *practical* question was whether the present state of affairs here would not be found unsatisfactory, and the climate hotter and less healthy than was desirable, or whether the luxuriant indications of opulence and ease I now beheld might not prove to be more captivating than expected, and the climate even more delightfully salubrious than I had dared to anticipate. I watched the lingering sunlight, wrapping the clouds, the mountains, and the sky into one glowing and refulgent scene, with all the enthusiasm of which my soul was capable; but the sun went quietly down, and the supper-bell reminded me of a fresh-caught mackerel. The sun and the land will come again to-morrow, but the mackerel disappeared forever.

Morning did come, and with it came the pilot (black). We entered the "port of silver" (Puerto del Plata). The harbor is a poor one; but if there be one thing on earth deserving the epithet "sublime," it is the surrounding scenery. We anchored, and there awaited the coming of the custom-house officers. The officers came—some white, some colored—and with them Mr. Collins, an American gentleman to whom I was addressed. He received me liberally, invited me to stop with him, promising to show me around the country, introduce me to the General, (black,) and do a variety of other things decidedly un-American, but very gentlemanly indeed.

It was Saturday afternoon when we went ashore,

and it so happened there was to be a government proclamation. In due time the drum struck up, and down came the standing army, looking for all the world like a parcel of ragamuffin boys playing militia. I counted them, and I think there were four drummers, two fifers, and two lines of soldiers —thirteen in a line. Some were barefooted, others wore shoes; some of their guns had bayonets, and others none. The manner in which they bore them compared with the foregoing suggestions, and so on to the end of this ridiculous scene. Dominicana has a government—so poets have empires.

In passing through the streets one is compelled to observe the non-progressive appearance of everything around him. There lie the unturned stones, just as they were laid a century ago. The houses are generally built one story high, with conical-shaped roofs, for no other reason than that that is the way this generation found them. Mr. Collins, who is a bachelor, lives in an airy two-story house, with a charming verandah running its whole length, cool and delicious, and surrounded by the sweetest fruit-trees outside of Eden. I found myself perpetually exclaiming, "Oh! what beautiful, bright roses!" what this, and what that, until I felt shamefully convicted of my own enthusiastic ignorance. I need not repeat the traveller's story, for the certainty of exposure is sure. Look at a wood-cut and say that you have seen Niagara, but don't read Harper's picture-books and suppose you have any idea of Haytien floral beauty.*

Of course I have not been here long enough to know whether it is a fit place for a man to live in, or for a number to colonize, and I am well aware, when the question of politics comes up, it turns on a very different pivot; but by all that is magnificent, lovely, exquisite, and delicious in its vegetable productions, I do set it down a perfect paradise.

---

* When the island was discovered by Columbus, it received from him the name of Hispaniola—" Little Spain." It was afterwards called Santo Domingo; but the original name given it by the natives, and revived by Dessalines, is said to be Hayti. The Haytien territory, however, is but about two-fifths of the island, the greater part being owned by the Dominicans.

LETTER II.

Dominican Republic.

WANT OF INFORMATION — ONE SIDE OF A QUESTION.

THERE is no school-boy but remembers, when tracing the history of Columbus on his perilous voyage across the sea in search of a new world, how eagerly he watched each favorable indication of bird or sea-weed, and ultimately with what rapture he greeted the joyous cry of land; nor who, looking back through the vista of centuries past, but brings vividly to mind the landing of Columbus, the simplicity of the natives, the cupidity of the Spaniards, and their insatiable thirst for gold. But further than this—further than a knowledge of a few of the most striking outlines of the earlier history of Hayti, or Hispaniola—there is generally known little or nothing; little of the vicissitudes and sanguinary scenes through which the peoples of this island have passed; nothing of the "easily attainable wealth almost in sight of our great commercial cities;" nothing of its sanitary districts peculiarly conducive to longevity. On the contrary, erroneous and exaggerated notions prevail, that because it is not within a given circle of isothermal lines it must necessarily be fit for the habitation only of centipedes, bugbears, land-sharks, and lizards. Indeed, it has been well said there is perhaps no portion of the civilized world of which the American people are so uninformed; and, in fact, so anomalous and apparently contradictory to the generally received impression does everything appear, that I almost despair of these papers being regarded as other than humorously paradoxical.

I am standing now on the line of 19° 45' of north latitude, or but 20° 15' south of the city of New York, and but 3° of longitude east, a distance not greater, I think, than by river from St. Louis to New Orleans, a distance frequently made by steamers within four days, and a distance which may be travelled over on railroads in the States at the rate of three times a week! Yet there are many persons who, were you to speak to them concerning this portion of the American tropics, you would find, regard it as being somewhere away on the coast of Africa, and the voyage hither long and tediously disagreeable. It is in reality but a small pleasure trip.

This is one side; but the great lesson of the

world's experience is that there are two sides to every question.

THE OTHER SIDE.

On the other hand, it may well be asked, if this be the Eden of the New World, why its flowers should be "born to blush unseen," and its "gems of purest ray" remain hidden in its hills; or, to speak less classically, why the country should lie so long a comparative *terra incognita*, producing generations of indolent men and women, excelling only in superstition, idleness, and profound stupidity. In the "Silver Port," the port in which we entered, vessels get within a quarter of a mile of land; then lighters take the cargo half the remaining distance, and from thence ox-carts convey it to the shore, when a comparatively small outlay of ingenuity, capital, and labor would make it a respectable harbor.

The men generally dress—those that dress at all—in cool white linen, Panama hats, and light gaiter boots. They look nice; but the red-turbaned, often bare-stockinged, loosely-dressed women are shocking.

> "Know then this truth, (enough for man to know,)
> Virtue alone is happiness below."

Soon after we arrived, a dark, brown-skinned, and as handsome a looking man as I ever saw, came on board as watchman. For my particular benefit, I suppose, the captain inquired if he had a wife; to which he replied, in broken Spanish, "Two—one is not a plenty."

A large portion of the cargo of the vessel in which I came consisted of lumber for the erection of a storehouse. The same vessel will be freighted back with timber of a superior quality. Indeed, the shores are lined with yellow-wood and mahogany; *but it is not sawed.* A gentleman is reported to have built a house in one of the interior towns which would have cost in Northern Ohio about $800, at a cost of $25,000. Inquire why this is so—why this listless inactivity prevails—and you receive the answer, "Well, waat is the use?" or, as Tennyson has it, "Vot's the hods, so long as you're 'appy." The "apathy of despair" has not reached here, but the apathy of stupidity is incurable.

CAUSES OF THE DECLINE OF THE SPANISH COLONY.

I am aware that many persons, among them our finest writers on "Civilization—Its Dependence on Physical Circumstances," attribute the cause of the island's decline from its ancient splendor, and the consequent supine indifference of the natives, to the effeminating influences attending all tropical climates; and, without prejudice, I believe such would be very greatly the case in a very large portion of the tropical world; but it is a libel on Hayti and Dominicana. The country is as healthy as Virginia, and, except in its excessive beauty and fertility, resembles much the state of North Carolina. "Nobody dies in Port-au-Platte," they say; but I should be sorry to find it true. I trace the cause in the country's history, as I think the following brief glance will show, for much of which I am indebted to W. S. Courtney, Esq., and his essay on "The Gold Fields of St. Domingo." We will say the civilized history of the country began with the Spaniards in 1492. The inhabitants, at the time of its discovery by Columbus, were a simple-minded, hospitable, and kind-hearted people, the fate (unparalleled suffering) of whom I have no disposition to record. The studious reader of American history will shudder at the bare recollection of the predatory scenes and excessively inhuman and bewildering iniquities of which they fell the victims, and which, if perpetrated now in any part of the world, " would send a thrill of horror to the heart of universal man." Montgomery, I think it is, expresses their fate touchingly, and in a nut-shell, thus :

> " Down to the dust the Carib people passed,
> Like autumn foliage withering in the blast ;
> A whole race sunk beneath the oppressor's rod,
> And left a blank among the works of God !"

The Spanish colonists brought with them, of course, the Spanish language, customs, laws, and religion, which language, customs, and religion prevail to this day. They were exceedingly prosperous through a long series of years. They built palatial residences, cultivated sugar and tobacco farms, erected prodigious warehouses, established assay offices, and worked the mines on a grand but unscientific scale. The mines are supposed to have yielded from twenty-five to thirty millions of dollars per annum, and the exports of sugar and other productions showed a corresponding degree of prosperity.

In about 1630 the island began to decline. The natives had been driven and tortured to the last degree, and the heroic Spaniards began to look around for other countries to conquer, other people to enslave. They discovered Mexico, Peru, and Brazil. The most glowing and captivating accounts went forth of the incalculable wealth of those countries in silver and gold, and multitudes abandoned their homes and haciendas and flocked thitherwards, in the hope of realizing wealth untold. Plantations and mines that had been producing immense revenues were abandoned to waste and desolation, and the population of the island was reduced one half from this one cause alone. Meanwhile, the French had established themselves on the western part of the island, and the present Haytien territory was ceded to France in 1773.

The remaining Spaniards introduced African slaves to supply the place of natives, and with this labor they were enabled to recover somewhat of their ancient thrift. Soon after this, the revolt in the French portion of the island occurred, and many of the Spanish slaves left the territory to join the standard of their revolutionary brethren. Besides this, whenever the French royalists drove the revolutionary forces back into the mountains, and cut off their supplies. the latter entered the Spanish territory, helped themselves to what they needed, destroyed the haciendas, carried off cattle and crops, and if they were resisted, as they sometimes were, they slaughtered the Spaniards as they do hogs in Cincinnati, Ohio, set the cities on fire.

and left behind a grand but terribly universal ruin.

The history of San Domingo was never completely written, and if it were, would never find a reader. But stand here on these shores, with a rising panorama of half the scenes enacted by these revolting and infuriated slaves, and there is not a planter in the Southern United States, who, for all the wealth Peru, Mexico, and St. Domingo could produce, would be willing to return home and remain there over night.

Finally, Dessalines, that extraordinary prince of cut-throats, entered the Spanish territory, slaughtered the French, laid waste the country for leagues, carried off the remaining slaves, and so bewildered and astounded the Spanish residents that they gathered up what movable wealth they could and left the country, "some for Mexico, some for Peru, while many returned to Spain."

Such are the principal and to me satisfactory causes which history assigns for the decline of the island's thrift, which had reached an unparalleled degree of prosperity and an unsurpassed grandeur and magnificence, with a rapidity unrivalled in the annals of the world.

SUBSEQUENT HISTORY.

For the gratification of your many readers, I will continue this homœopathic sketch of the island's history up to the present time.

In 1821 the Dominican portion (which embraces about three-fifths of the island, but having, I think, not more than one-fourth of its population) declared itself independent of the Spanish crown, but was shortly after subjugated by Boyer, the President of the Haytien Republic. In 1842 a revolution in Hayti caused Boyer to flee, and Riviere assumed the presidency. Two years after, the Dominicans overpowered Riviere, and on the 27th of February, 1844, reëstablished their government, or rather the present government of Dominicana. The main features of their constitution are, that each district or canton choose electors, who meet in preliminary electoral convention, and elect for four years the President and other administrative officers, and a certain number of counsellors, who constitute a congress.

The President, Pedro Santana, is a mixed blood of Spanish and Indian descent, and is emphatically regarded as a most estimable personage. Baez, the former President, is said to be of mixed French and African lineage; in short, there is no difference on account of color.

In 1849, Solouque, the President of Hayti, contrary to the wish of many Haytiens, undertook to conquer the Dominicans, and bring them unwillingly under his despotic sway. He entered the territory with five thousand men, but was met at Las Carreras, and disastrously defeated by General Santana, "with an army of but four hundred men under his command." This is the truth, or history is a lie.

For this brilliant achievement Santana received the title of "Libertador de la Patria," and seems to be admired, comparatively speaking, after the manner of our "liberator" and Father of his country. (Bah !)

But a small portion of the Haytiens, as I have before observed, sympathized with President Solouque in his abortive attempt to carry out the "Democratic" policy of territorial expansion. And when General Geffrard was proclaimed President, it is said the populace demanded pledges that he would not pursue the policy of his predecessor in this regard.

"It is not at all probable that any organized attempts of the Haytiens to recover possession of the Dominican territory will ever again be made; so that henceforth there will be no more annoyances of this sort." Such are the views and opinions of eminent men, who have given this subject some attention;* but in the opinion of the writer, as is generally known, the destiny of the island is union;—one in government, wants, and interest, brought about by the introduction of the English language, and by other peaceful and benignant mean; such language, wants, and interests to be introduced by the emigration hither of North Americans,—some white, but principally colored. England, France, and many other independent nations of the world, have acknowledged and formed liberal treaties with the weak little Republic, but I hope you do not suppose the government of the United States could be *guilty* of anything that looks like generosity.

God grant that I may never die in the United States of America!

---

* Within fifteen days a disaffection has been discovered near the Haytien frontiers, supposed to be the work of Solouque. Solouque is an imitator of Napoleon I. Napoleon went to Elba—Solouque to the island of Jamaica.

LETTER III.

Dominican Republic.

CORPUS CHRISTI.

BETWIXT midnight and daylight this morning I was lying sleeping and dreaming under the halcyon influences of the lingering land breezes, when suddenly a harmonious sound of partly brass and partly string instrumental music rang upon the air. It appeared just as music always does to any one in a semi-transparent slumber—not quite awake nor yet asleep—when, as everybody knows, it is sweet as love. One boom from the cannon, and I stood square on my feet; and, as it is not very remarkable here to see persons dressed in white, the next moment I was out on the verandah.

There went a jolly crowd, promiscuous enough, but apparently as light-hearted and happy as mortals get to be, and which to a slant-browed contriving Yankee is a poser. They had thus early begun to celebrate what is called *Corpus Christi*.

which, according to all fair translation, I should think means Christ's body. But any thing about it after that I am entirely unable to say. It would seem to require a good deal to understand all the Catholic ceremonies. Talk about their being ignorant! I never expect to learn so much while I live.

All business houses were closed for the day, and Dominican, French, American, and other colors were flying from their respective staffs. Altars were erected in various streets, with numerous candles burning within, and bedecked with particolored flags and flowers. They were really prettily and tastefully arranged. In short, it was an American 4th of July, except this: to each of these altars marched the throng of people headed by the priest. The priest said prayers in "Greek." The people *understood*, and all knelt down in the street, men, women, and children, but of course principally women.

THE FARM OF THE FUGITIVE SLAVE.

A party of us went out to see Mr. Smith, a fugitive slave, whose energy and well-directed enterprise had attracted some attention heretofore. He is not so fine looking a man as I expected to see. He is under five and a half feet in height, limps a little, and is altogether but little in advance, to use a most contemptible Americanism, of his "kind of people" in the States. He speaks no Spanish, and for that matter very little English; but he has a will of his own, and a determination to do something, which gives him an advantage over half a dozen persons who go to school to lose their common sense.

Mr. Smith was a slave in South Carolina; was brought by sea to Key West, and there hired out to work for a Republican government. He and some other of his fellow-slaves, including his wife, took sail-boat, set sail, and after suffering almost incredibly from sea-sickness and want of food, finally reached New Providence, which he had previously learned to be an English colony. He proceeded to declare his intention to become a British subject, and went to work; but wages being low, he concluded to remove to Dominicana and go to farming. He purchased a piece of land near the town of Porto Plata, and with the assistance of his "help-mate," (which in this country means a wife,) soon cleared the land of its tropical undergrowth, and planted it in corn and potatoes. In breaking up the ground he used a plow, a startling innovation here, but which produced most salutary results. A neighbor of his has since bought one. So great was the yield of Mr. Smith and his wife's crop that in little more than a year's time they have a house and forty acres of land all paid for, and a new crop worth over five hundred dollars, which will soon be ready for market.

This may not seem very remarkable to any one who has never seen a sand-hill, nor yet been to Canada; but to me it is a miracle. My object in mentioning this fact, however, is, to state that Mr. Smith also planted a few seeds of Sea-Island cotton, the product of which has been sent to New York and pronounced worth 14c. per pound. Now, there are numbers of colored men recently from the Southern States skilled in, and some who have made small fortunes by, the cultivation of cotton, at perhaps not more than eight or nine cents per pound, when, too, it had to be replanted every year. It produces here without replanting almost indefinitely, but it is safe to say seven years.

The query is this: give half a dozen such men as Smith a cotton-gin ($350), send them out here, and would they not accomplish more for the elevation of the colored race by the successful cultivation of cotton, in eighteen months. than all the mere talkers in as many years?

The meanest thing I have been obliged to do,

and the greatest sin I have committed, has been the registering my name as an American citizen. I presented myself to the United States consul (whose son and clerk, by the way, is a mulatto). The nice correspondence of Mr. Marcy was produced, not with any evil intent at all, but just to show what indefinable definitions there are between colored and black and white and negroes as American citizens. I should like to find out how a man *knows* he is an American citizen! There are members of Congress who can no more tell this than they can tell who are their fathers.

As for Mr. Corwin's talk about enforcing the laws, he may thank Heaven if he is not yet arrested as a fugitive slave.

Since the above was written, I understand the courts of Virginia have decided that an Octoroon is not a negro. Now, then, if an octoroon is not a *negro*, is an octoroon a citizen? And if an octoroon is not a negro, is a quadroon a negro?

LETTER IV.

Dominican Republic.

FIRST RIDE IN THE COUNTRY—PASTORISA PLACE.

"A YANKEE is known by the shortness of his stirrups;" so they say here, and I do not know that the criticism is at all too severe. Except Willis and one or two others, who of the Americans know any thing about riding? The Dominicans are good on horseback. In fact, it is their boast that they can ride or march further in two days than Americans want to go in a week. On the other hand, if "Los Yankees" had this country they would soon fix it so that a man could go over it all before the Dominicans got breakfast. Señor Pastorisa, (of the firm of Pastorisa, Collins & Co., formerly of St. Thomas,) who married a native, is mounted on a cream-colored horse, (cost $300,) and wears behind him a sword in a silver-gilt case. Every male person wears a sword of some kind, even though it prove to be as useless as an old case-knife. It is an old, superannuated, hundred-years-behind-the-age custom; yet in some instances serves as their Court of Appeals. No one disturbs you, and you are expected to be as well behaved; but if not, the difficulty is generally settled at the sword's point, and there it ends. How magnanimous even is this rude mode of settling disputes when compared to that of the one-sided, blaspheming, defrauding den of thieves called a court of justice in the States! Coming from a land where men kill each other without warning, instead of a sword which I would not know how to use, I buy a pair of holsters for horseman's pistols, throw them across the saddle, and am ready.

Now there may be no pistols in these holsters, of course, but what is the difference so long as they are supposed to be there? I take it as one of the grand lessons which the world's history teaches, that men are far more afraid of supposed and imaginary dangers than of those they know to be real. The number of backsliding sinners and snake-story witnesses are innumerable.

We were now at the base of the St. Mark's mountain, which rises just back of the town of Porto Plata. The so-called road was no road at all. There were little narrow trenches running between the rocks, fit for pack-mules, but scarcely wide enough to allow one's feet to pass. Up the mountain we came *poco á poco*. While passing these rocks the sun poured down with an intensity not previously experienced. But I had never been an alderman, and was not fat enough to melt; indeed, it might as well have shone on a pine knot. Ere long the sun hid behind a cloud, the thunder muttered a little, but pretty soon, as if by way of repentance, there came a restorative shower of tears. (Thank Heaven! the *nigger* question vanquished the sun.) Nothing is so calculated to make a man vain as a mountain shower. You enjoy its ineffable sensations yourself, while below you behold the poor valley fellows sweating in the sun. Or it may be they are drowning wet below, and you basking in the clear sunshine above. Either way, you are bound to rejoice and to look with contempt on the silly ones who make themselves miserable by regretting and whining over things that are in themselves unalterable, and need no change. The wise repine not.

Over the mountain and beside a stream, with limes scattered plentifully around, we stop a moment for refreshment. Lemonade is cheap, one would think; the limes are as free as the water. Had nature furnished the sweetening as well, we should have had a river of lemonade.

Here country settlements begin again, called *estancias*, which, if you will get a blackboard and a piece of chalk, I will explain. Mark off, say four acres of land, clear it up—let the fruit-trees stand, of course—enclose it, but plant nothing therein. In the centre of this piece erect a shanty. This much is called a *conuco*. Now go through the woods, say a mile and a half, clear up four acres more and plant tobacco. The next year or two this will be gone to weeds; you then (not knowing the use of a plow) go another half mile, clear up another piece and plant a new crop. The old place has gone to wreck, the new place is in its vigor; but neither is in sight of the house. This together is called an *estancia*, and I should have said before meant a farm, but it does not mean a farm in English by a good deal.

At this point we leave the "road," and, under full gallop half the while, take through the wood, guided by a dim path which winds over the hills and down the dales with as careless an indiscrimination as ever road was trodden by a prairie herd. L'Ouverture's feats or Putnam's celebrated escape would do to read about, but this was reducing the thing to practice.

Five miles' gallop over a level plain — thirty

miles in all—and we have reached Pastorisa Place: it is a perfect Arcadia.

During leisure moments I shall probably look back to this day's ride and to these enchanting scenes as one of the "gilt letter" chapters of my life; but at present, after a bath, the rapidity with which fried plantains, pine-apple syrup, and scorched sweet milk will disappear, would do a dyspeptic Northerner good to see!

The property comes by Señora Pastorisa. She is, perhaps, five-and-twenty. Her eyes are as bright and dark as even Lord Byron could have wished them to be. Her complexion is that of a clear ripe orange. The place is extensive, containing say nineteen thousand acres, in a valley five miles wide, fenced in on either side by a spear of mountains, with a limpid stream running through the centre. Mocking-birds enliven every thing; parrots and paroquettes go around in droves, screaming and squawking like a very nuisance. Back of the house is a grove appropriated to honey-bees. They swarm on every log. (There were certainly over one hundred swarms.) Honey is considered of but little value anywhere in the mountains, and is often wasted in the streams, the wax only being preserved. This comes of having pack-mules and goat-paths instead of wagons and wagon-roads.

Señor Pastorisa had informed me before of his desire to quit the town and improve his farm. All he needed was men who understood farming on the American plan. He has a plow, and intends harnessing an ox to-morrow to try the experiment of plowing. Now, it is clear that to plow the ground very successfully he will need at least a yoke of oxen—which he has, all but the yoke. This I would undertake to make, though I never did such a thing in my life, and always had a horror of an ox-yoke, anyway; but lo! there are no tools. So Señor Pastorisa needs hands, but with a very little *a priori* reasoning it will be seen there are other things needed quite as much. One is a road. There is a natural outlet to the valley—there must be. The stream before the door makes towards the Isabella river. The Isabella empties into the sea, of course.

I forgot to say Señora Pastorisa is "a little tinged"—the handsomest woman in the world.

LETTER V.

Dominican Republic.

VALLEY OF THE ISABELLA — CUSTOMS OF THE NATIVES — CHAPTER ON SNAKES — A CALL FOR DINNER.

> "Know ye the land where the cypress and myrtle
> Are emblems of deeds that are done in their clime;
> Where the rage of the vulture, the love of the turtle,
> Now melt into sorrow, now madden to crime;
> Where the flowers ever blossom, the beams ever shine,
> And all save the spirit of man is divine?"—BYRON.

THERE had been one or two invigorating showers previous to our ride down the valley of the Isabella, and so there remained a great deal of slippery clay along the narrow pathways, which paths lay usually on the very verge of some mountain slope, embankment, or more exciting precipice. To have come off with only one or two bones broken, I should have been perfectly satisfied.

We forded the river with impunity, crossed and recrossed it again, and finally came to as level a bottom plain as wheel ever rolled on. The valley of the Isabella is as handsome as a park.

The river itself is not so large as Longfellow's "Beautiful River," but it is much more deserving the name. Apropos, every old homestead has its particular title, such as the "Mocking-Bird," "Humming-Bird," "Crebahunda," and a variety of others for which there is no adequate translation. The legends attending them are frequently the most exquisite.

Considering, therefore, the remarkable history, exquisite legends, and extraordinary traditions of the country, I am bound to say, should there be sufficient emigration in this direction to produce a poet of the Hiawatha school, I should be sorry for the laurels of Mr. Longfellow. There are one or two parts of "Hiawatha," however, for which I hope to retain a relish.

The houses and cultivation along our way are in keeping with the *estancias* before described. The men are comparatively neat in appearance, find them where you will. The women are frequently good-looking, but seldom spirited. The prevailing question seems to be, How low in the neck can their dresses be worn? and the answer is, Very low indeed! White Swiss is worn as dress, and when seen on a handsome woman is like Balm of Gilead to the wounded eye. The wife does not usually eat at the table with her husband. She sees that his baths are ready, and at times even that his horse is fed, and at meal-times either takes her plate on her lap or awaits the second table. This is not from want of respect on the part of either; it is their stupid custom. Should "los Americanos" ever run a stage-coach up this valley, and two or three of these fellows have to climb on top for the sake of giving one lady an inside seat, they will comprehend somewhat better for whose convenience the world was made.

June 14th.—Señor Pastorisa fell ill to-day, and is now lying in a hammock. This gives me an opportunity to extol the hammock, which is too excellent a thing to pass unnoticed. It consists mainly of a net-work of grass, netted something like a seine, twice the length of a person or more, and fastened at the ends with cords sufficiently strong to hold the weight of any one. These cords are tied to the limb of a tree or the rafters of a house, and there you swing as happy as any baby ever rocked in a tree-top. It is sufficiently light to be carried in saddle-bag, and is altogether indispensable.

The señor's fever is also my excuse for pencilling down notes more minutely than I otherwise should. I can, of course, give you a description of but few things singly. The palm-tree ought to be one. This remarkable tree grows without a limb, smooth and regular as a barber-pole, from forty to sixty feet high. At this point it turns suddenly green, and puts out two or three shoots. Around these grow its berries, which are used for fattening pork. Each of these shoots furnishes monthly a rare peel or skin, which is used for covering houses, for packing tobacco, and for making bath-tubs, trays, and other articles of household furniture. The body of the tree is used for weather-boarding. It rives like a lath, the inside being pithy, somewhat like an elder. Its leaves are twelve feet long, and bend over as gracefully as an arch. In the centre of the top springs out a single blade, like the staff of a parasol. This was made (one would think) for mocking-birds to dance on. The most useful tree in the world, its usefulness is excelled by its own beauty.

The valley of the Isabella is a grove of palms.

One cannot but remark how preposterous are the snake stories which the vulgar relate respecting the West Indies and tropics generally. The world does not contain another thing so brazenly destitute of the least common sense. In all this rambling through the woods, over the hills, and along the streams, the most harmful thing I have seen is a honey-bee—not even a dead garter-snake!

While on board a vessel off the coast one day, a sailor threw overboard a hook and line, and in the course of time caught a young shark. It was as wicked a little thing as I ever saw, and strong as a new-born giant. The sailor struck it over the head with a stick, when it snapped the hook and flounced around the vessel. In short, he killed it, and proceeded to dress it for breakfast.

"Going to eat a shark?" I inquired.

"Why not?"

"Good heavens! I thought they were the worst things in the world."

"You eat duck," said he; "what's nastier than a duck? Shark's clean—swims in a clean sea."

I afterwards tasted a piece: it was coarse, and the idea that its mother might some day eat me, made the thing disgusting; but it learned me a lesson I shall not very soon forget. An Irishman is afraid to go to America on account of its frogs; a Frenchman makes a dish of them. One man eats rats, and another cats.

Now, to suppose there were no reptiles whatever in the country, or none peculiar to its bays and inlets, would be simply absurd; and when we get to the coast, I should be sorry to miss seeing some lazy old crocodile sunning in the sand. Should it have seven heads, however, I shall very likely catch it, and send it straight to Barnum; but if not, why, as Banks would the Union, let the snaky thing slide.

Your "Allergater in de brake" song may do for the Southern States, with their rhythmetical-and-stolen-from-the-African-coast slaves; but to apply it to this country would disgrace the most idiotic "What-is-it" ever imported. Of naturally wild quadruped animals there is not so much as a squirrel. Birds are without number.

Stanley is himself again! One and a half hours' ride, two fords of the river, (rising,) and we are at the mouth of the famous Isabella. The river is here, but the town of Isabella has passed away forever. The delta is covered with mahogany timbers; two schooners stand out in the distance awaiting to transport them to Europe; and with these exceptions—and with these alone, unless it be the absence of the Indians—were Columbus to arrive here again to-day, he would not find a particle more of improvement than was found here over three centuries and a half ago. A boat load of oarsmen coming down the river, the captain leading in a song, and all hands joining in the chorus; a splash is heard on the other side of the water, as if broken by a fish or clumsy sea-turtle; but except these sounds a death-like stillness pervades the entire valley.

To get a better view, you must cross the promontory (the northernmost point of the island) to where Columbus first landed. From thence you see the Haytien frontier stretching away in the dim blue distance, and the scene is enchantment.

Over the rocks we go, led on by a Spaniard on a little bay mule, that climbs over the cliffs with an agility creditable even for a mountain goat. The señor's horse falters. One misstep, and they both go to eternity!

We are on the beach. My zeal to commemorate the landing of Columbus by gathering a few tiny tinted shells reconciles the señor to sit in the sun and hold my horse for a minute; but I have no doubt he had rather see me as expert at gathering peas or picking up potatoes. "Ah! H.," says he, "leave off writing books and gathering shells; get married, and come to farming." So I will—all but the married.

But you will want to know what, after all, is the matter with the port. It is shallow. Vessels of a hundred tons burthen cannot get within as many rods of a harbor. In fact, the only question is, why a man of Columbus' sense ever stopped there at all. It is not worth the pen and ink it would take to describe it.

CALLED AT THE FIRST HOUSE FOR DINNER.

"Come, let the fatted calf be slain," was complied with to the very letter, except that in this instance it happened to be a *goat*. Nevertheless, it was worth the return of any prodigal son.

The largest "señorita" had a dress to make up. It was a piece of light blue delaine, and to her, no doubt, was "superb." She left off assisting the old patriarch in dressing the goat, walked to the pitcher, took the cocoanut dipper, and filled her mouth with water until her cheeks swelled out like a porpoise's. She then deliberately spirted it into her hands; and this was her mode of washing! She then spreads out her dry-goods, admires them a while, folds them up again, and lays them aside.

The four, and even six year old, running about the place, were as innocent of even a shirt as any son of Adam at his coming into the world.

We look out into the open, slab-sided kitchen, and see old and young sitting around on the dirt floor, enjoying a meal of fresh goat, winter squash, and plantain stewed together.

Our dinner is over; we bid these folks good-bye, and pronounce them the happiest set of miserably contented mortals the sun ever shone upon. Man needs excitement; he prays for ease.

We return to Pastorisa Place to spend the Sabbath. Two or three days of rest, and we start fresh again for Porto Cabello.

So ends the week—one at least in my life for which it was worth the trouble to have lived.

LETTER VI.

Dominican Republic.

ON THE WAY TO PORTO CABELLO—ANTILLE-AMERICANA—EMIGRATION ORDINANCE.

"Here in my arms as happy you shall be,
As halcyon brooding on a winter sea."
—DRYDEN.

WHEN the saffron sunlight lingers on the fleecy edges of these mountain clouds, there is a singular solemnity and peculiar fascination about them which can not be likened to any thing earthly. More than any thing else, the resemblance is that of a dark mourning-gown, lined with white satin and trimmed with silver tassels.

This reminds me that the sign of mourning here is somewhat novel. It is that of a spotless white kerchief worn on the head—a thing rarely seen, however, for the reason that people in this district rarely die except from sheer old age. There is near us an old man (black) whose entire grey hair and bodily appearance indicate his being at least eighty. His father died only a year ago, and for some time before the aged sire's death it is said that fires had to be kindled for him to sleep by, in order to generate sufficient heat to keep his thin, chilly blood in circulation. His age was beyond his own knowledge.

But the great object of life here seems to be that of eating. The first thing in the morning after leaving your hammock, you are furnished with a dish of aromatic coffee, strong and excellent as a beverage, and as little like the ordinary stuff you get at hotels as pure rich cream is like chalk and water. Bah! think of your dish-water slops, made of parched peas, and supposed to be West India coffee! Oh! nation of Barnums and egregious dupes!

Where circumstances allow it, not an hour in the day passes without something being brought in to be eaten. "This is an alligator pear—must be eaten with salt and pepper." Now it is honey, pineapple, mango, orange, banana, and even a joint of sugar-cane—anything to be eating. You are then expected to eat as hearty a dinner as ought to satisfy a man for a week. Ride a mile and a half and you are asked if you are not hungry. You reply, "No, indeed." Cross the next stream, and "Are you not thirsty?" is asked. Say "No, indeed" again if you like, and you will be very lucky not to hear your admirable self inelegantly compared to some kind of a goat.

The climate of these mountains seems to be that of perpetual spring, 88° Fahrenheit being the warmest day we have had so far. I understand, however, that in September the heat is much more oppressive because there are more calms, but never so intolerable as in the changeable latitudes. Sunstroke! You might venture the reputation of half a dozen "speakers" (a trade which is had in the States for the picking of it up) that such a thing as sunstroke would not be felt here until the world has wheeled as many years backward as it has forward.

We are trotting along on the way to Porto Cabello. I have given you a description of these valleys before, but passing a grove of *rose-apples* just now, (a fruit highly prized in the West Indies simply for its flavor, the tree being much like that of a lime, and the fruit hollow, something like a May-apple, lustrous as an orange, and flavored precisely as a rose is perfumed,) I could but reflect that if another Eve were to be placed in an earthly garden I should pray that it might be somewhere among the hills of New England, for, doubtless, then she would meet temptation with a masterly resistance; but if placed in such a garden as might be made in this country,—with all the sins of the world before her I fear she would be tempted over again a thousand times.

Stop a moment on an elevated point of a homestead called "Crebchunda;" behold the grand valleys stretching away between the mountain chains until lost in the green-blue sea which the glass shows in the distance. Dodging under branches, going sometimes head-first through the eternal verdure which, if possible, grows even more luxuriant, in this way we ultimately reach Porto Cabello, a place which proves to be, as previously understood, the grandest point for a port of entry on the whole northern coast of the island.

These old Spaniards are all the time saying to me,

"My son, you never look pert."

"Perfectly happy, uncle," I reply.

"Look long time away—studying."

"Nothing, uncle—only an American."

"Only an American? Well, what do they different from other people?"

"Lay out towns one day, and build them the next; own lands, and improve them."

Now, this is genuine American talk; whether it will be American practice remains to be seen.

Porto Cabello is now used to some extent as a point of export; but the only reason why it is not used more extensively is, that between this and the valley there is a hill to be crossed, which could be made respectable as a highway by six sturdy hands in as many days. The country is ripening for immigration. Mr. James Redpath, a talented English-American, and a most acute observer, recently traversed a portion of the Haytien territory, and came to the conclusion that the entire island was capable of sustaining 20,000,000 people. There is not upon it probably one million, and of these the greater portion are in Hayti. The Dominican territory, by far the most extensive and desirable, does not contain much over one-fourth of a million, all told.

I say the country is ripening for immigration. The Pike's Peak fever will ere long be exhausted. Then there is, probably, no more promising field for enterprise than this in the entire new world. Most any point could be made to flourish by the opening of good roads. With Porto Cabello this is peculiarly so. Santiago is the principal interior town. It is the proper place for, and was the former capital. It is situated on the river Yaque, which courses La Vega Real, (the Royal Plains,) and contains about 12,000 inhabitants. The trade of Porto Plata is kept alive mainly from this source; but the mountainous road between them, over which nothing can be transported except by piecemeal on horseback, has been well-nigh the ruin of them both. Porto Cabello is sixteen miles west of Porto Plata. It shuns the St. Mark's mountain, and it is fair to suppose that, could communication once be established between this and Santiago, and were there the least facilities here for shipping produce, the trade of the interior would inevitably flow in this direction. As to the shipping interest, it was that which first turned our attention hither; for Porto Plata being an unsafe harbor for the winter, vessels had been known to make this port for safety. There are nine feet of water on the shallowest bar, and this once over there are two quiet bays, in either of which a merchantman could ride without an anchor.

There will be an American settlement up this valley,—the nucleus where I now stand, and this their port of entry. Such a settlement would meet the encouragement of Señor Pastorisa, and, as I have reason to believe, of the natives generally. They have no labor-saving machines, which is, beyond all question, what the country most needs. Think of a community like this getting on without a plow, a cotton-gin, a saw-mill, or anything of the kind. It is, verily, astounding. There is, of course —and it is certainly natural enough—a lingering prejudice against white Americans. This may or may not be overcome; but the natural question is, Are colored men in America competent to infuse the spirit of enterprise which the country demands? *Let the common-sense working-men answer.* My experience with your "leading" would-be-white-imitating upstarts is conclusive.

The route—and a cheap one—is from New York to Porto Plata. Agricultural implements are admitted duty free. I send herewith an important communication, showing the disposition of the government towards immigration. It is easy to see that (if carried into effect) it will mark a new epoch in the country's history.

But before this question is taken into the debating rooms—that is, the pulpits—for discussion, it ought to be understood. If people read Homer's poetic descriptions of imaginary scenery, and come here expecting to find them realized, they will be fully as much disappointed as they deserve. There are times when the clouds rise slowly over the mountain height, with a blazing sun at their backs, when the skies glow with a splendor transcending all conception; yet it is not at all likely they will see these mountains "go bobbing 'round," or "nodding," to suit the convenience of anybody. Must mountains necessarily rest their exalted heads against the bosom of the sky, as if holding constant *tête-à-tête* communion with the stars? If so, there are no mountains here—nothing but potatoe-ridges. Nor will they be blindly dazzled by the excessive resplendence of the sun or moon; nor will the moon make silver out of anything upon which it may happen to shine. Moonshine is moonshine, I suppose, the world over. American poets, however, may be read with impunity.

> "This is the land where the citron scents the gale;
> Where dwells the orange in the golden vale;
> Where softer zephyrs fan the azure skies;
> Where myrtles grow, and prouder laurels rise."

IMMIGRATION ORDINANCE.

The following is a translated copy of an important official paper published in San Domingo city, June 9th, and proclaimed in Porto Plata, June 28, 1860:

"Antonio Abad Alfare, General of Division, Vice President of the Republic, and entrusted with the executive power, looking at the necessity which exists for facilitating the execution of the laws concerning immigration, defining the manner of making effective the measures which the government may take for their observance, the council of Ministers having heard, has come to issue the following ordinance:

"ART. 1. That there be constituted a Board of Immigration in each capital of a province, and in the qualified ports of Samana and Puerto Plata. These shall be composed of four members named by His Excellency, among those most friendly to the progress of the country, of the Governor of the provincial capital, or the Commandant-at-Arms in the communes, who shall be the president of them. Their secretaries shall also be of said commission.

"ART. 2. These Boards shall meet at the seat of government in the provincial capital, and in the communes of Puerto Plata and Samana, at the Commandant-at-Arms. For their internal ordering and the more ready fulfilment of that which is assigned them, they shall regulate that which they have to do according to utility, first submitting it for approval to the Minister of the Interior.

"ART. 3. The functions of the Board are: First, to learn the easiest and cheapest way of bringing immigrants to the country, always communicating everything to the President through the Minister of the Interior. Second, to employ all means leading to the result that there shall only come as immigrants the agricultural class, or those following some craft, profession, or useful form of labor; to get information of lands belonging to the nation most suitable for health and fertility; to have them prepared to furnish to farmers who may not have been able to agree with private individuals under the terms of their contracts; to assign them lodgings and sustenance after their arrival, during a period to be agreed on, and to look after them with all the attention and care which it shall be possible to display; to supply them with tools and other articles of use which it may be decided to furnish to them, and with the first stock of seed-corn for their sowing, taking care that everything be of the best quality; to take care that those who agree with private persons shall be under a contract which insures the fulfilment of that which has been agreed with them; to attend to all things which can give credit to this department as well within as without the Republic.

"Art. 4. The Board shall appoint agents for the furnishing of victuals to those who shall be needy, taking care that in every thing there be exactness, order, and good faith.

"Art. 5. All accounts of expenses which may

actually be incurred must be examined and approved by the Board, and submitted to the inspection of the Minister of the Interior.

"ART. 6. The office of member of the Board is honorary, and without pay, and they shall perform their functions two years. Those who perform with zeal and patriotism their trust, will be entitled to the esteem and consideration of their fellow-citizens.

"ART. 7. The present ordinance will be promptly executed by the Ministers of the Interior, Police, and Agriculture.

"Given at St. Domingo City, the capital of the Republic, the 4th day of June, 1860, and the 17th year of independence.

"A. ALFAU.

"Countersigned, the Minister Secretary of State, in the departments of justice and education, charged with those of the interior, police, and agriculture.

"JACINTO DE CASTRO."

LETTER VII.

Dominican Republic.

PROPOSED AMERICAN SETTLEMENT—PICTURE OF LIFE—TOMB OF THE WESLEYAN MISSIONARY.

"Thy promises are like Adonis' garden—
That one day bloomed, and fruitful were the next."
—KING HENRY VI.

I HAVE scarcely time to inform you of an American settlement really begun. It is near the sea, not far from Porto Plata, on a large *commonality* or tract of land embracing about twelve square miles, (not twelve miles square,) having a water power running full length. The land being in common is considered of the first importance, for by this means a small outlay of capital—say one hundred dollars—secures to the settler the grazing advantage of the whole tract, where not otherwise in use. This idea was suggested by an eminent gentleman of St Louis, and has been the custom of early settlements in Spanish colonies for centuries past. It will of course be subdivided whenever desired, each man taking the part he had originally improved. The principal settlers are from Massachusetts, one of whom, a Mr. Treadwell, (colored,) designs establishing a manual-labor school. Another, a Mr. Locke, (white,) who came out for his health, has actually secured a mill site, erected a small shanty, and cleared from twelve to twenty acres of land, as preparatory steps towards building a saw-mill. How happy will be the effect of such enterprise on a non-progressive people you have probably anticipated from what I have previously observed.

The manual-labor school is, without question, the only mode of infusing a tone of morality in the country, or giving a foothold to the Protestant religion. This has been tried. About twenty years ago a society of Wesleyan Methodists established a mission in the town of Porto Plata. The church still lives, and is, by foreigners, comparatively well attended; but they have not converted a single Catholic by preaching from that day to this. The reason is, the Catholics will not go to hear them. Yet, for the benefits of an education, about one hundred and fifty children were sent regularly to school, and there, by the "infidel" teachings of the Wesleyans, they soon learned to distrust the ceremonies of their mother church. Unfortunately, about two years since this school was discontinued, and, having succeeded in weaning the people from positive Catholicism without yet embracing the Protestant religion, it seems to have left them with a general belief in every thing, which is, as I take it, the nearest point to a belief in nothing.

The country around Porto Plata is owned almost entirely by the Catholic church, being leased, through the government, at reasonable rates to such persons as desire to settle thereupon; but by establishing a school at a distance of seven miles, as above indicated, it would be entirely free from all such influences. An English missionary is soon to come over from one of the neighboring islands to give the location his personal inspection.

The sea view is divine. Along the shallow edges the rippling waves appear brightly green—greener than the trees—while beyond this, where the water deepens, the hue is a pearly purple—purer purple than a grape. In fact, the earth does not contain a comparison for the tranquil beauty of this transparent sea. Some hours ago I thought to sketch it for you, lest it should prove, like so many other things, too fine to last; but so it continued hour after hour, and until the sun nestled in its very heart.

So much for the future settlement. It may be

called "Excelsior," but at present I will call it "Crebahunda."

This cool morning air nearly chills me. You take a bath and retire to bed at night with only a thin linen sheet spread over you. In the morning you are chilled, and resolve to sleep hereafter under more covering; but, of course, when night comes again you do not need any more.

Not a morning, my dear H., do I look upon these fields of living green but that I think of you and your daily routine of office duties. I take a seat beneath one of these forbidden-fruit trees while the land breeze is freighting the valley with perfume, the sun just peeping over the hills, and the white mists, beautiful as a bridal veil, slowly rising up the mountain green; now listening to the voice of a favorite mock-bird, and then to the softer cooings of a mourning-dove. A strange-looking little hummy perches on the first dead limb before me. Parrots squawk, and a dozen blackbirds chime one chorus, while other varieties chirp and trill. The whole scene is Elysian. Then along comes a sparrow-hawk, and choo-ee! choo-ee! choo-ee! off they all go, helter-skelter.

Of whom is this a picture? You are toiling

away, arranging rude manuscripts, at times almost discouraged, but still toiling on in your close, hot rooms—and this for the good of your race. Well, Heaven grant they may thank you for it, and save you from crying at last, "Choo-ee! choo-ee!" But, ah!—even worse than that—I am afraid the sparrow-hawks will catch you! With me, the end of every thing is that of the birds—a melancholy aggravation. I have been entranced by these morning scenes but a passing short while, and will soon be compelled to leave them and take a lonely ride to the coast, thence to depart for a season. I therefore stuff my saddle-bags with oranges and cinnamon-apples, as I think this is wiser than weeping.

An absence of precisely four weeks, and we are once again in sight of Porto Plata. "The moon is up, and yet it is not night." Some kind of a holiday being at hand, men, women, and children are riding to and fro up and down the streets on donkeys, mules, and ponies of every description. The scene is truly picturesque. I could but remark to my friend the Protestant exhorter, the grandeur of the evening, to which he replied, "A man that could find fault with this climate would find fault with Paradise." I do not believe him, however, for whether the day and night trips along the coast have been too much for me or not, I have certainly got the chill-fever.

This morning, July 7th, I visited the tomb of the Wesleyan missionary to whose labors here I have before referred. The following inscription will furnish the data to such of your readers as are interested in the history of such missions:

IN MEMORY

OF THE

REV. WM. TOWER,

WHO WAS BORN AT HORNCASTLE, LINCOLNSHIRE, ENGLAND, ON THE 12TH FEBRUARY, 1811, AND ENTERED UPON THE MISSIONARY WORK OF EVANGELIZING THIS ISLAND IN

1838.

HE LABORED ON THIS STATION FOURTEEN YEARS AND A HALF. HE WAS BELOVED BY ALL WHO KNEW HIM; AND DIED ON THE 25TH OF AUGUST,

1853,

UNIVERSALLY REGRETTED.

LETTER VIII.

Dominican Republic.

SUMMARY OF STAPLES, EXPORTS, AND PRODUCTS.

"I CAME across a copy of Rousseau this morning," said an American scholar, whom we had met before; and he added, "I should not have been more surprised had I seen it drop out of the clear sky."

There are but very few books in Dominicana of any kind, and no reliable statistics. The government on the south side of the island appoints custom-house officers on the north side, allowing them little or nothing for their services. The consequence is, these officers pay themselves out of the import duties, and hence few returns are accurately made.

In the essay on the "Gold Fields of St. Domingo,"* to which I have previously referred, I find the following summary of staples, exports, and products, which, while it is but little more than the

---

* Published by A. P. Norton, New York.

reader will have already gathered, may serve at least to confirm what has been said:

"The chief products of the Dominican part of the island are now mahogany, tobacco, indigo, sugar, hides, bees-wax, cocoa-nuts, oranges, lemons, some coffee and some fustic, satin and many other kinds of wood; but the trade in those articles now is not very considerable. There is a vast quantity of *mahogany* in the territory, standing in groves on the mountains and the plains, and scattered over the valleys and along the rivers and streams. The best mahogany in the West Indies grows on this island. Some of these groves and trees are truly magnificent, growing straight and to a great height. The best is now found inland, as it has been nearly all already stripped off the coasts and cut away from near the mouths of the principal rivers and around the bays, where it was more accessible and of easier and cheaper carriage to market. It has been extensively used for building purposes by the inhabitants of the cities, more especially by those of the interior, the lumber now used in the coast cities being carried thither from the States, and exchanged for mahogany and other products. It is only of late years that the best mahogany cuts have begun to come to market, as heretofore they were carried to Europe, where they brought a better price.

"*Tobacco* is now one of the principal exports. But little of it, however, finds its way to this market. There is a large quantity of it raised by the residents on the Spanish part of the island, particularly about Santiago, on the Royal Plains, and in the neighborhood of Macerere. It is brought down in bales or ceroons on mules to Port Platte, and shipped on board Dutch bottoms to Holland and the Germanic states. There is also some cultivated about St. Domingo City and around the Bay of Samana. But the cultivation and traffic in this commodity compared with what it might be, were those fertile plains and rich savannahs settled by an industrious and enterprising people, is scarcely as a drop to the bucket. There are regions in the territory where tobacco can be grown equal to the best Havana brands, and, on account of the fecundity of the soil, with even much less labor.

"There are still some good *sugar* plantations in the Dominican territory, chiefly about St. Domingo City and to the west as far as Azua, but they are 'few and far between.' The best sugar is now produced in the region about Azua and Manuel, and is of a very superior quality. The country people cultivate and manufacture, each on his own account, and, in his small way, pack it in ceroons and carry it down to the coast on mules. Indeed, the term 'cultivate' is not appropriately used in this connection, as the cane grows up wild and spontaneously from season to season, and from year to year in many places, and the inhabitants have nothing whatever to do but cut and grind it in wooden mills and boil day after day. The writer is not informed that they use the sugar-mills in use in other sugar-growing countries in their operations. It is easy to conceive what a source of incalculable wealth the culture of this staple there would become, if in the hands of a skilful and enterprising population.

"The trade in *hides*, compared with other products, is quite important, which arises from the fact that a majority of the population pursue grazing for a livelihood, and the rapidity with which stock increases and the little care required in preserving it. Owing to the heat and abundant oxygen which the atmosphere contains, the flesh of the beef, unless properly salted and cured, keeps but a day or two, so that the inhabitants are obliged to kill almost every other day. This now keeps up and supplies the traffic. Perhaps three-fifths of the population of the interior country and towns are now engaged in grazing.

"Compared also with other staples, the trade in *bees-wax* is considerable. The island producing the greatest quantity and variety of flowering plants, shrubs, and trees, bees exist there in incalculable and immense swarms. The prairies of the West in June furnish no parallel to the flowers that perpetually unfold on these mountains, plains, and valleys. The writer has been informed by a gentleman who recently visited Dominica [Dominicana], that so strong and rank was the odor from the flowers in passing over the Royal Plains, that it so jaded his olfactories as to cause his head to ache, and almost made him sick. The swarms build in the rocks, in the trees and logs, under the branches, and even on the ground. Those who pursue this branch of business collect the deposits in tubs, wash out the honey in the brooks by squeezing the combs, and afterwards melt the wax into cakes, or run it into vessels preparatory to carrying it to market. Those engaged in this vocation are chiefly women. The trade in this article, however, bears no proportion to its production and abundance. They have recently begun to save some of the honey, and a small quantity of it has found its way to this market.

The reason why it has not been hitherto saved is owing to the great cost of vessels to collect it in, as wooden-ware of all kinds has to be taken there from the States.

"There are some exports of *cocoa-nuts*, *oranges*, *lemons*, *limes*, and other fruit, all of which are both cultivated and grow wild in vast abundance on the island, and are not excelled by any in the Antilles, or on the Spanish main. The labor necessary to collect them, prepare them for shipment, and carry them to the ports is not there. From this cause, indeed, the whole Spanish end of the island languishes in sloth, and its transcendent wealth goes year after year incontinently to waste.

"There is some *coffee*, which grows wild in abundance through the island and on the mountains, and is collected and shipped. After the abandonment of the coffee plantations, the trees continued to grow thick on them, and finally spread into the woods and on to the mountains, where they now grow wild in great quantities. Lacking the proper culture, its quality is not the best, but the climate and soil is capable of producing it unexcelled by any in Porto Rico or any of the West Indies or Brazil. The writer is informed, however, that there are a few coffee plantations under culture about St. Domingo City. The labor of cultivating coffee and sugar in Dominica [Dominicana], with all the modern appliances of civilization, would be absolutely insignificant compared with the rich returns it would bring the planter.

"In addition to the staples and exports above-mentioned, the island produces a vast number of other valuable commodities, among which we may make notable mention of its lumber and different varieties of valuable wood other than mahogany. The pitch or yellow pine grows in vast abundance at the head of the streams and on the mountains, dark and apparently impenetrable forests of which cover their sides and tops. This lumber, with very little expenditure of labor and capital, could be brought down the streams during their rises almost any month in the year, to the principal cities. When the reader is made acquainted with the stubborn fact that all the lumber used on the north side of the island, except the little mahogany that is sawed there and at and about St. Domingo City, is carried there at great cost from the States, and sold at a price fabulous to our lumber-dealers here, he will measurably comprehend the undeveloped resources of Dominica [Dominicana] in that interest alone. Pine lumber sells at Port Platte for $60 per thousand feet. It has then to be carried back to Santiago, Moco, and La Vega on mules, where it sells for $100 per thousand, while those mountains and the banks of their streams stand thickly clothed with it, in its majestic and sublime abundance! There is but one saw-mill on the Spanish end of the island near St. Domingo City, and that not now in operation. They saw by hand a little mahogany at a cost of 80 cents a cut, ten feet long; and when an individual wishes to build a house at Santiago, Moco, La Vega, Cotuy, or any of the interior towns, he has to begin to collect his lumber a year beforehand!... In consequence of this scarcity and cost of lumber, those of smaller means build their floors of brick and flags, and roof their houses with the same material or with the leaf of the palm-tree. Besides the pine, there is the oak, the fustic and satin woods, compache, and an indefinite variety of others. Some of the hardest and most durable vegetable fibre in the world is to be found on the island."

It may appear somewhat strange to the reader that mahogany should be used for building purposes, but so it is. The art of veneering is but little known, house furniture consisting generally of solid mahogany.

LETTER IX.

Republic of Hayti.

HISTORICAL SKETCH — GENERAL DESCRIPTION PREVIOUS TO 1790.

"Think not that prodigies must rule a state—
That great revulsions spring from something great."

I HAVE given you Dominicana as a garden of poetry and the home of legendary song. Well, Hayti is a land of historical facts, and the field of unparalleled glory. Consulting one day with Mr. Redpath, the talented author of the series of letters to which I have previously referred, he suggested the impossibility of any one forming even a comparatively correct opinion respecting affairs in Hayti, without being guided by a sketch of the country's previous history. Confessedly, therefore, much as his letters were appreciated by the readers of the *Tribune* he had not done the Haytiens simple justice. Since nothing could be so highly interesting, be it mine and the *Anglo-African's* to undertake what the *Tribune* and its correspondent failed to supply. The following compilation will be taken from Rainsford's, St. Domingo, and Edwards' and Coke's histories of the West Indies, but principally, and when not otherwise marked, from Coke.

There is nothing low or cowardly in the history of Hayti. Notwithstanding their conquests on the main land, the Spaniards were wont to regard it as the parent colony and capital of their American possessions. The buccaneers of Tortuga, however much they may have suffered or have been feared, can not be said to have ever been really conquered. In fact, by whomsoever settled, the country has shown one uninterrupted record of pride and independence. I regard this as an honor to begin with.

The history of Hayti begins with the buccaneers, a company of French, English, and Germans, driven from their homes in the neighboring islands by the haughty arrogance of the Spaniards, in 1629. These men, collected on the shores of Tortuga, vowed mutual fidelity and protection to each other, but eternal vengeance against their persecutors. How well they kept their word has passed into a proverb.

In 1665 the court of Versailles, observing a beautiful country of which some of its subjects had taken an actual though accidental possession, took the fugitive colony under its protection. It was not difficult for the French government to see that the island was in value equal to an empire, and it was therefore determined to enhance its interests with all possible speed. The first care was to select a governor who should be equal to the difficult task of humanizing men who had become barbarians; which important task was committed to D'Ogerton, a gentleman of Anjou.

Hitherto not a single female resided in the settlement, to supply which deficiency was the governor's first care. With this view he sent immediately to France, and many women of reputable character were induced to embark. From this time the prosperity of the colony fairly begins.

The personal fame of D'Ogerton drew many who had suffered persecution at home to flee for safety to an asylum which his lenient measures had established in Hayti, among whom was one Gobin, a Calvinist, who, upon his arrival, (1680,) erected a house on the Cape, and prevailed on others to join him in his retreat. Time added to their numbers, and the conveniences of the situation justified their choice. As the lands became cleared and the value of its commodious bay became known, both inhabitants and shipping resorted to the spot, and raised the town of Cape François to a degree of elegance, wealth, and commercial importance which in 1790 scarcely any city in the West Indies could presume to rival.

Considered in itself, the situation of the town is not to be commended. It stands at the foot of a very high mountain which prevents the inhabitants from enjoying the land breezes, which are not only delicious but absolutely necessary to health. It also obstructs the rays of the sun, causing them to be reflected in such a manner as to render the heat at times almost insupportable. On one side of the town, however, is an extensive plain, containing, perhaps, without any exception, some of the finest lands in the world. The air is temperate, though the days and nights are constantly cool. In short, it is another Eden. "Happy the mortal who first taught the French to settle on this delicious spot."

The situation of Port au Prince, to which place the seat of government has been transferred, seems to have been unfortunately selected. It is low and marshy, and the air is impregnated with noxious vapors, rendering it extremely unwholesome. To this day it is commonly regarded as the graveyard of American seamen. In 1790 it had also reached an eminent degree of prosperity, and contained 14,754 inhabitants, of whom 2,754 were white, 4,000 free people of color, and the remainder slaves. So, also, near Port au Prince is a fertile plain called Cul de Sac. The mountains surrounding it possess a grateful soil, and are cultivated even to their summits. The value of such lands is at present from ten to twenty dollars per acre.

The town of St. Mark's, near which the last body of colored emigrants from America have settled, is somewhat more advantageously situated. It lies on the northern shore of the bay, on the point of an obtuse angle formed by the margin of the rocks and waves. Hills encircle it in the form of a crescent, the points of which unite with the sea, and, while they afford it shelter, leave it open to the breezes of the ocean, which become the springs of health.

The land which the French had brought under cultivation previous to the revolution was devoted mostly to the cultivation of sugar, coffee, indigo, and chocolate. It is said that Hayti alone produced as much sugar at this time as all the British West Indies united. The prodigious productions of little more than two million acres of land were as follows: brown sugar, 93,773,300 lbs.; white sugar,

47,516,351 lbs.; cotton, 7,004,274 lbs.; indigo, 758,628 lbs. But great as this product may appear, it by no means gives the entire amount, the quantity of tanned hides, spirits, &c., being equally immense.

Immorality and irreligion everywhere prevailed, worse even than at present, if we are to judge from a poem written about that time. The West Indies would seem to be peculiarly conducive to this species of iniquity:

> "For piety, that richest, sweetest grant,
> Of purest love blest super-lunar plant,
> Is here neglected for inferior good,
> Torn from the roots, or blasted in the bud.
> Soft indolence her downy couch displays,
> And lulls her victims in inglorious ease,
> While guilty passions to their foul embrace
> Seduce the daughters of the swarthy race."

This brings us to the consideration of the all-important subject called in America the "negro question," but which is, nevertheless, the immortal question of the rights of man.

The inhabitants of Hayti consisted of 540,000 souls, and were divided into three distinct classes —the whites, the slaves, and the mulattoes and free blacks. The term mulatto comprehended all shades between whites and negroes. The whites conducted themselves as if born to command, and the blacks, awed into submission, yielded obedience to their imperious mandates, while the mulattoes were despised by both parties.

The freedom they enjoyed was rather nominal than real. On reaching a state of manhood each became liable to serve in a military establishment, the office of which was to arrest runaway slaves, protect travellers on the public roads, and, in short, to "mount a three years' guard on the public tranquillity." To complete their degradation, they were utterly disqualified from holding any office or place of public trust. No mulatto durst assume the surname of his father; and to prevent the revenge which such flagrant and contemptible injustice could hardly fail to excite, the law had enacted that if a free man of color presumed to strike a white man, *his right arm should be cut off*. In fact, they were not much above the condition of the free blacks in the United States. "On comparing the situation of these two classes of men"—the slaves and the nominally free—says Coke, "it is difficult to say which was the most degraded. The social difference was, without doubt, very great, but in the aggregate must have been about the same."

Such was the state of affairs previous to 1790. What they have been subsequently remains to be seen. The whip of terror never yet made a friend. It may prevent men from being avowed enemies for a while, but it usually makes a deeper impression upon the heart than upon the skin. The heart is nearest the seat of recollection, and will stimulate to revenge for a long time after the wound has been inflicted, as the reader of the following pages will abundantly attest.

"Time the Avenger! unto thee I lift
My hands and eyes and heart, and crave of thee a gift."

LETTER X.

Republic of Hayti.

AFFAIRS IN FRANCE—THE CASE OF THE MULATTOES—TERRIBLE FATE OF OGE AND CHAVINE.

IT was towards the close of the year 1788 that the revolutionary spirit which had been fermenting among the French people from the conclusion of the American war first manifested itself in the mother country; and although that extraordinary event convulsed the empire in every part, in no place was the shock so great as in Hayti.

The mulattoes, notwithstanding their oppression and degradation, it should have been observed, were permitted to enjoy property, including slaves, to any amount, and many of them had actually acquired considerable estates. By these means the most wealthy had sent their children to France for education, just as many are now sent to Oberlin, in which place they supported them in no small degree of grandeur.

It happened about this time that a considerable

number of these mulattoes were in Paris, among whom was Vincent Ogé. This young man entered into the political questions relative to the people of color, which were then violently agitated, and became influenced with a conflict of passions at the wrongs which he and his degraded countrymen were apparently destined to endure. His reputed father was a white planter, of some degree of eminence and respectability, but he had been dead for years. Ogé was about 30 years of age; his abilities were far from being contemptible, but they were not equal to his ambition, nor sufficient to conduct him through that enterprise in which he soon after engaged. Supported in Paris in a state of affluence, he found no difficulty in associating with La Fayette, Gregorie, and Brissot, from whom he learned the prevailing notion of equality, and into the spirit of which he incautiously entered with all the enthusiasm and ardor natural to the youthful mind when irritated by unmerited injuries; and he determined to avenge his wrongs.

Induced to believe that all the mulattoes of Hayti were actuated by the same high-minded principle, he sacrificed his fortune, prepared for hostilities, and sailed to join his brethren in Hayti.

What was Ogé's disappointment when, after

evading the vigilance of the police and secretly succeeding in reaching these shores, he found no party prepared to receive him, or willing to take up arms in their own defence! It probably might have been said of him also, "*His heart is seared.*"

About two hundred were at length prevailed upon to rally around his standard; and with this inadequate force he proceeded to declare his intentions, and actually dispatched a note to the governor to that effect.

In his military arrangements his two brothers were to act under him, with one Mark Chavine, as lieutenants. Ogé and his brothers were humane in their dispositions, and averse to the shedding of blood; but with Chavine the case was totally different.

Ferocious, sanguinary, and courageous, he began his career with acts of violence which it was impossible for Ogé to prevent.

Finally the brothers of Ogé joined Chavine in his petty depredations. White men were murdered as accident threw them in their way. The mulattoes, when they could not be induced to join them, were treated with every species of indignity; and one man in particular, who excused himself from joining them on account of his family, was murdered, together with his wife and six children.

The inhabitants of Cape François, alarmed at these outrages which they imagined to be committed by a far more formidable body of revolters than really existed, immediately took measures for their suppression.

A detachment of regular troops invested the mulatto camp, which, after making an ineffectual resistance in which many were killed, was entirely broken up. The whole troop dispersed. Ogé and his officers took refuge in the Spanish part of the island. The principal part of their ammunition and military stores immediately fell into the hands of the victors.

The triumphs of the whites over the vanquished insurgents were such that they proceeded from victory to insult. The lower orders especially discovered such pointed animosity against the mulattoes at large that they became seriously alarmed for their personal safety, and many regretted not having joined the now vanquished party.

Urged by fatal necessity many resorted to arms, so that several camps were formed in different parts of the colony far more formidable than that of Ogé.

At this time RIGAUD, the mulatto general, makes his appearance, declaring that no peace would be permanent "until one class of people had exterminated the other."

In the midst of these commotions which presaged an approaching tempest, PEYNIER, the governor, resigned his office in favor of general Blanchelande. The first step of the latter was directed towards the unfortunate Ogé. The demand made on the Spanish governor for his arrest was peremptory and decisive. Twenty of Ogé's followers, including one of his brothers, were speedily hung; but a severer fate awaited Ogé and Chavine. They were condemned to be broken alive, and were actually left to perish in that terrible condition on the wheel.

Chavine, the hardy lieutenant, met his destiny with that undaunted firmness which had marked his life. He bore the extremity of his torture with an invincible resolution, without betraying the least symptom of fear, and without uttering a groan at his excruciating sufferings.

With Ogé the case was widely different. When sentence was passed upon him his fortitude abandoned him altogether. He wept; he solicited mercy in terms of the most abject humility; but in the end he was hurried to execution, and left to expire in the most horrid agonies.

Previous to this the National Assembly in France, which had originally declared " That all men are born free, and continue free and equal as to their rights," had to contradict this in order to pacify the planters, and to declare it was not their intention to interfere with the local institutions of the colonies.

It so happened, however, that with this decree they also transmitted to the governor a chapter of instructions, one of the articles of which expressed this sentiment: " That every person of the age of twenty-five and upwards, possessing property or having resided two years in the colony and paid taxes, should be permitted to vote in the formation of the colonial assembly." It was like the Dred Scott decision of the United States, for the question immediately arose whether the term " every person " included the mulattoes.

It was just at this time that intelligence of the tragical death of Ogé, who had been previously well known in Paris, reached that city. The public mind was instantly inflamed against the planters almost to madness, and for some time those in the city were unable to appear in public, either to apologize for their brethren or defend themselves. To keep alive that resentment which had been awakened, a tragedy was founded on the dying agonies of Ogé, and the theatres of Paris conveyed the tidings of his exit to all classes of people.

Brissot and Gregorie, two well-known reformers, availing themselves of this auspicious moment, brought the case of the mulattoes before the National Assembly.

This was early in May, 1791. The eloquence displayed by Gregorie on this occasion was most marvellous, enforced by such facts as a state of slavery and degradation rarely fails to produce, and the whole finished by an affecting recital of the death of Ogé.

Amid the ardor with which he pleaded the cause of the mulattoes, a few persons attempted to stem the torrent by predicting the ruin of the colonies. "*Perish the colonies,*" exclaimed Robespierre in reply, "rather than sacrifice one iota of our principles." The sentiment was reiterated amid the applauses of an enthusiastic Senate, and the National Assembly, on the 15th day of May, decreed that the people of color born of free parents should thenceforth have all the rights of

French citizens; that they should have votes in the choice of representatives, and be eligible to seats both in the parochial and colonial assemblies.

The colonial representatives no sooner heard that these decisive steps were taken than they declared their office useless, and resolved to decline any further attempts to preserve the colonies.

The colonists who resided in the mother country heard the decree with indignation and amazement. But in the island, as soon as it became known, the planters sunk into a state of torpor, and appeared for a moment as if petrified into statues. All local feuds between the whites were immediately suspended, and all animosities swallowed up by what appeared to them an evil of unparalleled magnitude. The civic oath was treated with contempt; tumult succeeded subordination; proposals were made to hoist the British colors; and resolutions crowded on resolutions to renounce at once all connection with a country that had placed the rights of the mulattoes on an equal footing with their own.

The mulattoes, who became criminal from their color, were obliged to flee in every direction. Their homes afforded them no protection. They were threatened with shooting in the street; and thus menaced by destruction, they began to arm in every direction.

The governor beheld this commotion with palsied solicitude. He foresaw the evils that must burst upon the colony, without having it in his power to apply either a preventive or a remedy.

But a far more awful mine, surcharged with combustibles, and destined to appall all parties, was at that moment on the very eve of an explosion.

LETTER XI.

Republic of Hayti.

A CHAPTER OF HORRORS (WHICH THE DELICATE READER MAY, IF HE CHOOSES, OMIT).

> "Out breaks at once the far-resounding cry—
> The standard of revolt is raised on high."

AMONG the various transactions which had taken place, both in the island and in France, little or no attention had been paid to the condition of the slaves. It is true an abolition society had been early established in Paris, called the "Friends of the Blacks," (*Amis des noirs*.) Their sufferings had also been used to give energy to a harangue, or to enforce the necessity of general reformation, but their situation was passed over by the legislative assemblies as a subject that admitted of no redress.

These, sensible of their condition, numbers, and powers, resolved, amid the general confusion, to assert their freedom and legislate for themselves.

They had learned from the contentions of both their white and colored masters that violence was necessary to prosperity. Such measures they adopted; and no sooner adopted than they were carried into effect.

It was early on the morning of August 23, 1791, that a confused report began to circulate through the capital that the negroes were not only in a state of insurrection, but that they were consuming with fire what the sword had spared. A report so serious could not fail to spread the greatest alarm. It was credited by the timid, despised by the fearless, but was deeply interesting to all. Pretty soon the arrival of a few half-breathless fugitives confirmed the melancholy news; they had just escaped from the scene of desolation and carnage, and hastened to the town to beg protection and to communicate the fatal particulars. From these white fugitives (the scale had turned) it was learned that the insurrection was begun by the slaves on a plantation not more than nine miles from Cape François.

There, it appeared, in the dead of night, they had assembled together and massacred every branch of their master's family that fell in their way. From thence they proceeded to the next plantation, where they acted in the same manner, and augmented their number with the slaves whom the murder of their master had apparently liberated. And so on they went, from plantation to plantation, recruiting their forces in proportion to the murders they committed, and extending their desolations as their numbers increased.

From the plantation of M. Flaville they carried off the wife and three daughters, and three daughters of the attorney, after murdering him before their faces. In many cases the white women were rescued from death with the most horrid intentions, and were actually compelled to suffer violation *on the mangled bodies of their dead husbands, friends, or brothers, to whom they had been clinging for protection.*

The return of daylight, for which those who had escaped the sword anxiously waited, to show them the full extent of their danger, was anticipated by the flames that now began to kindle in every direction. This was the work of but a single half night. The shrieks of the inhabitants and the spreading of the conflagration, occasionally intercepted by columns of smoke which had begun to ascend, formed the mournful spectacle which appeared through a vast extent of country when the day began to dawn.

It was now obvious that the insurrection was general, and that the measures of the revolted slaves had been skilfully preconcerted, on which account the revolt became more dangerous. The blacks on the plantation of M. Gallifet had been treated with such remarkable tenderness that their happiness became proverbial. These, it was presumed, would retain their fidelity. So M. Odelac, the agent of the plantation, and member of the General Assembly, determined to visit them at the head of a few soldiers, and to lead them against the insurgents. When he got there he found they had not only raised the ensign of rebellion, but had actually erected for their standard THE BODY OF A WHITE INFANT, *which they had impaled on a stake.* So much for happy negroes and contented slaves! Retreat was impossible. M. Odelac himself was soon surrounded and murdered without mercy, his companions sharing the same fate—all except two or three, who escaped by instant flight only to add their tale to the list of woes.

The governor proceeded immediately to put the towns in a proper state of defence; and all the inhabitants were, without distinction, called upon to labor at the fortifications. Messengers were despatched to all the remotest places, both by sea and land, to which any communication was open, to apprise the people of their danger, and to give them timely notice to prepare for the defence. Through the promptitude with which the whites acted, a chain of posts was instantly established and several camps were formed.

But the revolt was now found to be even greater than imagined. The slaves, as if impelled by one common instinct, seemed to catch the contagion without any visible communication. Danger became every day more and more imminent, so much so that an embargo was laid on all the shipping, to secure the inhabitants a retreat in case of the last extremity. Among the different camps which had been formed by the whites were one at Grande Riviere and another at Dondon. Both of these were attacked by a body of negroes and mulattoes, and a long and bloody contest ensued. In the end the whites were routed and compelled to take refuge in the Spanish dominions. Throughout the succeeding night carnage and conflagration went hand in hand, the latter of which became more terrible from the glare which it cast on the surrounding darkness. Nothing remained to counteract the ravages of the insurgents but the shrieks and tears of the suffering fugitives, and these were usually permitted to plead in vain.

The instances of barbarity which followed are

too horrible for description; nor should we be induced to transcribe any portion of them, were it not that many persons regard such statements as mere assertions unless accompanied by a record of the unhappy facts. The recital of a few, however, will set all doubts forever at rest.

"They seized," says Edwards, "a Mr. Blenan, an officer of the police, and, having nailed him alive to one of the gates of his plantation, chopped off his limbs one by one with an axe."

"A poor man named Robert, a carpenter, by endeavoring to conceal himself from the notice of the rebels, was discovered in his hiding-place, and the negroes declared that he *should die in the way of his occupation;* accordingly they laid him between two boards, and deliberately sawed him asunder."

"All the white and even the mulatto children whose fathers had not joined in the revolt were murdered without exception, frequently before their eyes, or while clinging to the bosoms of their mothers. Young women of all ranks were first violated by whole troops of barbarians, and then, generally, put to death. Some of them, indeed, were reserved for the gratification of the lust of the leaders, and others had their eyes scooped out with a knife."

"In the parish of Timbe, at a place called the

Great Ravine, a venerable planter, the father of two beautiful young ladies, was tied down by the savage ringleader of a band, who ravished the eldest daughter in his presence, and delivered over the youngest to one of his followers. Their passions being satisfied, they slaughtered both the father and the daughters."

"M. Cardineau, a planter of Grande Riviere, had two natural sons by a black woman. He had manumitted them in their infancy, and treated them with great tenderness. They both joined the revolt; and when their father endeavored to divert them from their purpose by soothing language and pecuniary offers, they took his money, and then stabbed him to the heart."

Amid the worst of these scenes Mr. Edwards records that solitary and affecting instance wherein a *soft-hearted* slave saved the lives of his master and family by sending them adrift on the river by moonlight.* This is generally admitted to have been the *Washington* of Hayti, Toussaint L'Ouverture.

At this time, also, the mulatto chiefs, actuated by different motives, not only refused to adopt such

---

* For a beautiful description of this affecting scene, see Whittier's "Toussaint L'Ouverture."

horrid measures, but particularly declared their only intention in taking up arms was to support the decree of the 15th of May, which had acknowledged their rights, of which the whites had been endeavoring to deprive them, and proposed to lay down their arms provided the whites acknowledged them as equals.

The white inhabitants gladly availed themselves of an overture which, though it pressed hard on their ambition, afforded a prospect for deliverance from impending danger. A truce immediately took place, which they denominated a *concordat*. An act of oblivion was passed on both sides over all that had passed, the whites admitting in all its force the decree giving equality to the mulattoes. The sentence passed upon Ogé and the execution of it the *concordat* declared to be infamous, and to be "held in everlasting execration." So much for Ogé.

Both parties now appeared to be equally satisfied, and a mutual confidence took place. Nothing remained but to induce the mulattoes to join the whites in the reduction of the negroes, now in a most formidable state of insurrection. To this the mulattoes consented. New troops were introduced from France. The whites were elated, and perfect tranquillity stood for a moment on the very tiptoe of anticipation.

But the great lesson of the revolution was speedily to be learned. The hurricane of terror which was yet to overcome them was at that moment on the Atlantic, and hastening with fatal impetuosity towards these uncertain shores.

UNION.

It was early in the month of September that intelligence reached France of the reception which the decree of the 15th of May had met with in Hayti. The tumult and horrid massacres which we have noticed were represented in their most affecting colors. Consequences more dreadful were still anticipated. The resolution of the whites never to allow the operation of the ill-fated decree was represented as immovable; and serious apprehensions were entertained for the loss of the colony.

The mercantile towns grew alarmed for the safety of their capitals, and petitions and remonstrances were poured in upon the National Assembly from every interested quarter for the repeal of that decree which they plainly foresaw must involve the colony in all the horrors of civil war, and increase those heaps of ashes which had already deformed its once beautiful plains.

The National Assembly, now on the eve of dissolution, listened with astonishment to the effects of a decree which, by acknowledging the rights of the mulattoes, it was expected would cover them with glory. The tide of popular opinion had begun to ebb; the members of the Assembly fluctuated in indecision; the friends of the planters seized each favorable moment to press their point, and actually procured a repeal of the decree at the same moment that it had become a medium of peace in Hayti.

At length the news reached these unhappy shores. The infatuated whites resolved to support the repeal, which would leave the mulattoes at their mercy. A sullen silence prevailed among the latter, interrupted at first by occasional murmurings and execrations, and finally exploding in a frenzy which produced the most diabolical excesses yet on record.

Rigaud's original motto was again revived, and each party seemed to aim at the extermination of the other. The mulattoes made a desperate attempt to capture Port au Prince, but the European troops lately arrived defeated them with considerable loss. They nevertheless set fire to the city, which lighted up a conflagration in which more than a third part of it was reduced to ashes.

Driven from Port au Prince, by the light of those flames which they had kindled, the mulattoes established themselves at La Croix Bouquets in considerable force, in which port they maintained themselves with more than equal address. At last, finding themselves and the revolted slaves engaged in a common cause, they contrived to unite their forces, and with this view drew to their body the swarms that resided in Cul de Sac. Augmented with these undisciplined myriads they risked a general engagement, in which two thousand blacks were left dead on the field; about fifty mulattoes were killed, and some taken prisoners. The loss of the whites was carefully concealed, but is supposed to have been equally as destructive.

The furious whites seized a mulatto chief whom they had taken prisoner, and, to their everlasting infamy, upon him they determined to wreak their vengeance. They placed him in a cart, driving large spike nails through his feet into the boards on which they rested to prevent his escape, and to show their dexterity in torture. In this miserable condition he was conducted through the streets, and exposed to the insults of those who mocked his sufferings. He was then liberated from this partial crucifixion to suffer a new mode of torment. His bones were then broken in pieces, and finally he was cast alive into the fire, where he expired. So much for the whites.

The mulattoes, irritated to madness at the inhumanity with which one of their leaders had been treated, only awaited an opportunity to avenge his wrongs. Unfortunately, an opportunity soon occurred. In the neighborhood of Jerimie, M. Sejourne and his wife were seized. The lady was materially *enciente*. Her husband was first murdered before her eyes. They then ripped open her body, took out the infant and *gave it to the hogs;* after which they cut off her husband's head and entombed it in her bowels. "Such were the first displays of vengeance and retaliation, and such were the scenes that closed the year 1791."

> "A law there is of ancient fame,
> By nature's self in every land implanted,
> *Lex Talionis* is its latin name ;
> But if an English term be wanted,
> Give our next neighbor but a pat,
> He'll give you back as good and tell you—*tit for tat!*

LETTER XII.

Republic of Hayti.

TRAGEDY OF THE REVOLUTION CONTINUED — RIGAUD SUCCEEDED BY TOUSSAINT—TOUSSAINT DUPED BY LE CLERC.

WE omit, as unnecessary to the thread of this narrative, the contentions between the French and English, in consequence of the British invasion, from 1792 to 1798; during which time Rigaud was succeeded by Toussaint L'Ouverture, whose superior military genius had won for him the appointment of Commander-in-Chief of the native forces.

But there is yet another "lesson of the hour" to be gleaned from the history of this marvellous revolution. Treachery led to the fall of Toussaint.

On the 1st day of July, 1801, a Declaration of Independence was made by Toussaint, in the name of the people.

The ancient proprietors of plantations, who in the former insurrections had been compelled to quit the island and seek an asylum in France, soon found in this act of independence a confirmation of their former suspicions. They saw that all their valuable possessions must be inevitably lost, and that forever, unless government could be prevailed on to send an armed force to crush at once a revolt which had become so formidable as to assume independence.

The complicated interests of commerce were instantly alarmed and awakened to action; powerful parties were formed; a horde of venal writers started immediately into notice; a change was wrought in the public sentiment as by the power of magic; and negro emancipation was treated in just the same manner that negro slavery had been treated before. Such was the fickleness of the French at that time, and such is the inconstancy of the human mind in ours.

Bonaparte, aiming himself at uncontrolled dominion, found it necessary to bribe all parties with gratifying promises to induce them to favor his views, and to enable him to introduce such changes in the form of government as he desired.

The transitory peace which had taken place in Europe produced at this time a band of desperate adventurers, who, destitute of employment, were ready for any enterprise that could afford them an opportunity to distinguish themselves. Accordingly an expedition of 26,000 men was fitted out, at the head of which was placed General le Clerc;* and such was the confidence of its success, that he was accompanied by his wife, (sister to Napoleon,) and her younger brother Jerome Bonaparte.

But it was not to the fleet and army that Napoleon trusted exclusively for success. A number of plotting emissaries had been secretly dispatched to tamper with the unsuspecting blacks, to sow the seeds of discord between parties, and to shake their confidence in Toussaint. Even Toussaint's children had been prepared, by the deceitful caresses of the First Consul, to assist, by their representation of his conduct towards them, in the seduction of their father.

Le Clerc with his detachment of the French squadron, appeared off Cape François on the 5th day of January, 1802. General Christophe, who, during the absence of Toussaint, held the command, on perceiving the approach of the French fleet, immediately dispatched one of his officers to inform the commander of the squadron of Toussaint's absence, and to assure him he could not permit any troops to land until he had heard from the General-in-Chief. "That in case the direction of the expedition

* Rainsford.

should persist in the disembarkation of his forces without permission, he should consider the white inhabitants in his district as hostages for his conduct, and, in consequence of any attack, the place attacked would be immediately consigned to the flames.".

The inhabitants, trembling for their personal safety and the fall of the city, sent a deputation to assure Le Clerc that what had been threatened by Christophe would actually be realized should he persist in his attempt to land his forces.

Le Clerc, regardless of this destiny, and intent upon the gratification of his own ambition, proceeded to put on shore his troops, flattering himself with being able to gain the heights of the Cape before the blacks should have time to light up their threatened conflagration.

Christophe instantly perceived this movement, and, steady to his purpose, ordered his soldiers to defend themselves in their respective posts to the last extremity, and to sink if possible the ships of the assailants; but that when their own positions were no longer tenable, to remove whatever valuables could be preserved, reduce every thing besides to ashes, and retire.

Le Clerc did not reach the heights of the Cape

until evening, and then only to behold the flames which Christophe had kindled, and which filled even the French soldiers with horror. They beheld with unavailing anguish the stately city in a blaze, the glare of which gilded the ceiling of heaven with a dismal light. Their expectation of a booty vanished in an instant, and the only reward which awaited them, they plainly perceived, was a heap of ashes or a bed of fire.

It was during these scenes of devastation on the shores that Toussaint was engaged in rendering the interior as formidable as possible; after the accomplishing of which he returned towards the ruins of the capital to discover if possible the real intentions of the French respecting the island, and to learn if any amicable proposition was to be made, which should secure to the inhabitants that freedom for which they had taken up arms.

In this moment of suspended rapine, Le Clerc resolved to try what effect a letter addressed personally to Toussaint by Napoleon would have upon the black commander, who was yet unapprised of its existence, or of the arrival of his sons from France. A courier was immediately dispatched with the former, and with intelligence that the latter were with their mother on his plantation, called Ennerry.

The wife and children of Toussaint, ignorant of the part they were to play, entertained, as the author of their happiness, Coison, the preceptor of their children, who was at that moment plotting their destruction.

Toussaint, animated with the feelings of an affectionate parent, hastened, on the receipt of the letter and intelligence of the arrival of his children, to fold them in his warm embrace. He reached the plantation the ensuing night. When his arrival was announced, the mother shrieked, and instantly became insensible from a delirium of joy. The children ran to meet their father, and sunk without utterance into his open arms. When the first burst of joy was over, and the hero turned to caress him to whom he immediately owed the delight he had experienced, Coison began his attack. He recapitulated the letters of Bonaparte and Le Clerc; he invited him to accede to them, and represented the advantages resulting from his submission in such glowing colors as could hardly fail to awaken some suspicions. He perfidiously declared that the armament was not designed to abridge the liberty of the blacks, and concluded with observing that, unless the proposed conditions were immediately acceded to his orders were to return the children to the Cape.

Toussaint retired for a few moments from the presence of his wife and children, to weigh the import of their common supplication. His awakened reason instantly discovered the snare which had been laid to entrap him, and he therefore indignantly replied: "Take back my children, if it must be so; I will be faithful to my brethren and my God!"* then, mounting his horse, rode off to the camp, from which place he returned a formal answer to Le Clerc.

Unfortunately Le Clerc's bribery was not so ineffectual in other quarters. Many of Toussaint's generals were induced to listen to the promises of Le Clerc, and

"To sell for gold what gold could never buy."

Among these was an officer named La Plume, who by his treachery threw a large district into the hands of the French, and also revealed to them those plans of operation with which Toussaint had entrusted him.

Such an act on the part of La Plume, in whom

* Rainsford.

Toussaint had placed unlimited confidence, could not but cause him to distrust those who remained attached to the common cause; and who, perceiving these suspicions, grew lax in the obedience which they owed to his commands.

On the 24th of February a severe battle took place between the French troops under General Rochambeau, and those under General Toussaint, consisting of 1,500 grenadiers, 1,200 other chosen soldiers, and 400 dragoons. The position of the blacks was extremely well chosen, being in a ravine fortified by nature and protected by works of art. Rochambeau, availing himself of his local knowledge of the country, which he had obtained from La Plume, entered the ravine with as much address as Toussaint could have manifested, avoided the obstacles which had been thrown in his way, and commenced an attack on the entrenchments of the blacks. Toussaint was prepared to receive him, and a desperate battle ensued, in which both skill and courage were alike conspicuous. The day was extremely bloody, and the field which victory hesitated to bestow on either party was covered with the bodies of the slain. Both parties at the close of the day retired from the scene of action to provide rather for their future safety than to renew a fierce contention for a mere point of honor.

Rochambeau hastened with the remains of his division to join the French troops in the western province, who were unable to withstand the force of the black General Maurepas. The troops thus collected were put in action, and the doubtful issue of battle was expected to decide their fortune. But Le Clerc had recourse to his usual manœuvres, and Maurepas, seduced with the promise of retaining his rank under the auspices of Le Clerc, submitted to the French general without a struggle, and gave his posts into the enemy's hands.

Le Clerc, finding he could conquer the blacks much more readily by winning their confidence than by swords, redoubled his efforts in this direction. The number of his emissaries was increased; their powers were enlarged, and they were sent forth as the missionaries of seduction to induce the unsuspecting inhabitants to put on their chains. Success in proportion to his professions attended their exertions. Even Christophe was induced to believe that the late proclamations, in which Le Clerc promised liberty to all, were sincere. And, finally, Toussaint, willing to prevent the effusion of blood, gave way to the representations of Christophe, who immediately entered into correspondence with Le Clerc.

A truce was formed on the ground of an oblivion of the past, the freedom of the men in arms, and the preservation of his own rank, that of Toussaint and Dessalines, and all the officers in connection with them. This proposition was made by Christophe, and agreed to by Toussaint; but Dessalines, dreading such an unnatural compromise, submitted only under protest. The proposals, after some hesitation on the part of Le Clerc, were accepted.

Hostilities ceased on the 1st of May.

Not one month past before Le Clerc seized Toussaint, his family, and about one hundred of his immediate associates, and placed them as prisoners on board the vessels then lying in the harbor. Many of the blacks were ordered to return to their labors under their ancient masters.

Toussaint, amazed at such an act of treachery and baseness, inquired the cause, but could obtain no other reply than that he must instantly depart. For himself he offered no excuse, declaring that he was ready to accompany his abductors in obedience to his orders; but as his wife was feeble and his children helpless, he begged earnestly that they might be permitted to remain. His expostulations were of course urged in vain.

Le Clerc, to rid the island for ever of a man

whom he both feared and detested, prepared, soon after the capture of Toussaint, to send him to Europe, and with him a letter of accusation at once false, criminal, and malicious. A letter more dishonorable never crossed the Atlantic. Upon his arrival in France, Toussaint was immediately sent to prison in a remote province in the interior, and entirely secluded from the society of men.

Shut up in melancholy silence, in a dungeon horrid, damp, and cold, his suffering was not long. The Paris journals of April 27, 1803, say this— no more and no less: " Toussaint died in prison."

As to his wife and children, they remained in close custody at Brest for about two months after their only friend was torn from them. They were then removed to the same province in which Toussaint had been imprisoned, without knowing anything either of his proximity or his fate. In this place, reduced to distress, they continued neglected and forgotten, a sad spectacle of fallen greatness.

Such was the fate of Toussaint L'Ouverture, the *Washington*, but not " *the Napoleon*," of Hayti.

LETTER XIII.

Republic of Hayti.

THE WAR RENEWED—"LIBERTY OR DEATH"—EXPULSION OF THE FRENCH — THE AURORA OF PEACE — JEAN JACQUES DESSALINES, FIRST EMPEROR OF HAYTI — PRINCIPAL EVENTS UP TO PRESENT DATE — GEFFRARD AND EDUCATION — POSSIBLE FUTURE.

> "This is the moral of all human tales;
> 'Tis but the same rehearsal of the past—
> First freedom, and then glory."
> —CHILDE HAROLD.

THE violent and perfidious measures to which Le Clerc had resorted produced an effect diametrically opposed to that which he intended. On the distant mountains, particularly toward the Spanish division, innumerable hosts of blacks had taken up their residence and assumed a species of lawless violence. They ridiculed every idea of a surrender to the Europeans, notwithstanding the compromise which had been made with Toussaint and Christophe. Even among those who had submitted, the sudden seizure of their brave leader and about one hundred of his enlightened associates, of whose fate they could receive no satisfactory account, but who was supposed to have been murdered by Le Clerc, produced a spirit of indignation which was poured forth in execrations portending an approaching storm.

Le Clerc, seated on his painful eminence, saw in a great measure the danger of his situation, and endeavored to counteract the impending evil. But death at this moment was lessening the number of his troops, and sickness disabling the survivors from performing the common duties of their stations.

Dessalines, whose talents and valor, recognized by his countrymen, had caused him to be appointed to act as General-in-Chief, resolved not to dally with his faithless foes as Toussaint had done, but to bring this ferocious war to a speedy and decisive issue. Impressed with this resolution, he drew a considerable force into the plain of Cape François, with a design to attack the city. Rochambeau, perceiving his movements, exerted himself to strengthen the fortifications of the city, after which he determined to risk a general engagement.

Both parties were as well prepared for the event as circumstances would admit. The attack was begun by the French with the utmost resolution, and from the violence of the onset the troops of Dessalines gave way for a moment, and a considerable number fell prisoners into the hands of the French.

But the power and courage of the blacks soon returned. The French were repulsed; and as a body of them were marching to strengthen one of the wings of their army, they were unexpectedly surrounded by the blacks, made prisoners of war, and driven in triumph to their camp.

With these vicissitudes terminated the day. At night the French general, to the disgrace of Europe, ordered the black prisoners to be put to death. The order was executed with circumstances of peculiar barbarity. Some perished on the spot; others were mutilated in their limbs, legs, and vital parts, and left in that horrible condition to disturb with their shrieks and groans the silence of the night.

But Rochambeau had to deal with a very different man from Toussaint—a man whose motto was, "*Never to retaliate;*" for under cover of the same inauspicious night Dessalines deliberately selected the officers from among his prisoners, then added a number of privates, and gibbeted them all together in a place most exposed to the French army.

Nor did the revenge of the black soldiers terminate even here. Burning with indignation against the men whose conduct had stimulated them to such inhuman deeds, they rushed down upon the French the ensuing morning, destroyed the camp, made a terrible slaughter, and compelled the flying fugitives to take refuge under the walls of Cape François. From this period the French were unable to face their opponents in the open field, and the victorious Dessalines immediately took steps to crush them in the city.

To add to the calamities of the French commander, the war between England and France was again renewed during this period of his distress. Unfortunately, however, he remained uninstructed by past experience, and his cruelty seemed to increase with the desperation of his circumstances. Pent up in the city, from which his forces durst not venture in a body, he contrived to detach small parties with bloodhounds to hunt down a few straggling negroes, who wandered through the woods unconscious of the impending danger. These when taken were seized with brutal triumph, and thrown to the dogs to be devoured alive.

Amid scenes and horrors as infamous as these, Le Clerc was summoned by the fever to appear before a higher tribunal to give an account of his deeds of darkness. He died on the 1st of November, after having been driven from Tortuga, his previous place of abode. Madame Le Clerc was present at the awful scene; then, departing with the body for Europe, bade a final farewell to a region which had promised her happiness, but paid her with anguish and mortification.

It was in the month of July that an English squadron, not fully apprised of the condition of the French army, made its appearance off the cape. This circumstance completely overwhelmed the besieged commander, who, while the blacks were fiercely crowding upon him, was perfectly conscious of his vulnerable condition as exposed to the British. He therefore opened a communication with the latter to learn what terms of capitulation he had to expect in case a proposition of that kind should be made. The terms required by the British being dreadfully severe, Rochambeau lost no time in strengthening the works towards the sea as well as towards the land, having every thing to fear from both quarters.

Meanwhile the victorious blacks continued to pour in reinforcements upon the plains of the cape. A powerful body now descended upon the French, and, having passed the outer lines and several blockhouses, prepared to storm the city in thirty-six hours.

Rochambeau, from a persuasion that all would be put to the sword, proceeded before it was too late to offer articles of capitulation, which, to the honor of Dessalines, by foregoing the desire of revenge, were accepted, granting the French ten days to evacuate the city—"an instance of forbearance and magnanimity," says Rainsford, "of which there are not many examples in ancient or modern history."

The articles of capitulation which Rochambeau had entered into were communicated by Dessalines to the British commodore. The latter, therefore, awaited the expiration of the appointed time to mark the important event. When the time had elapsed, Commodore Loring, perceiving no movement of the French towards evacuation, sent a letter to General Dessalines to inquire if any alteration had taken place subsequent to his last communication, and if not, to request him to send some pilots on board to conduct his squadron into the harbor to take possession of the French shipping. To this letter he received the following characteristic reply:—

"LIBERTY or DEATH!

"HEAD-QUARTERS, *Nov*. 27, 1803.

"*The Commander-in-Chief of the Native Army to Commodore Loring, etc., etc.:*

"SIR:—I acknowledge the receipt of your letter, and you may be assured that my disposition toward you and against General Rochambeau is invariable.

"I shall take possession of the cape to-morrow morning at the head of my army. It is a matter of great regret to me that I cannot send you the pilots which you require. I presume that you will have no occasion for them, as I shall compel the French vessels to quit the road, and you will do with them what you shall think proper.

"I have the honor to be, etc., etc.,

"DESSALINES."

Scarcely had Commodore Loring entered the harbor on the morning of the 30th, before he was met by an officer of the French troops then going in quest of the English to request them to take possession of the ships in the name of His Britannic Majesty. This, he observed, was the only method left by which they could be saved from inevitable destruction, as the black general was at that moment preparing to fire upon them with red-hot shot, and the wind, blowing directly into the mouth of the harbor, prevented their departure.

The whole of the French troops and shipping, including seventeen merchant vessels and about 8,000 soldiers and seamen, thus falling into the hands of the British, were conveyed to England, arriving at

Portsmouth on the 3d of February, 1804, from whence the troops were taken into the interior and paroled as prisoners of war.

Thus ended this visionary expedition through which Napoleon and Le Clerc flattered themselves and the country that the inhabitants of Hayti were to be again reduced to slavery; and thus, by the unrelenting determination of Dessalines, were the fearful thunderbolts of war made to recoil on the heads of those who hurled them.

THE AURORA OF PEACE.

The "Aurora of Peace" which Dessalines and his colleagues had predicted, was now ushered in. On the 14th of May following Dessalines departed from the cape, determined, like his unfortunate predecessor Toussaint, to make a tour through the island, to note the manners which prevailed, and to observe how far the regulations he had already introduced were enforced, and what beneficial effects had resulted from their adoption.

During this journey the people, animated by the presence of their victorious chief, resolved to exalt him to the dignity of emperor. Whether any intrigue had been used on this occasion by Dessalines, or that the offer was a pure emanation of gratitude originating with the people, it is impossible to say. This much, however, is certain, that the proposal was accepted without any reluctance, and in due time he was enthroned as *Jean Jacques Dessalines, the first emperor of Hayti*. This was at Port au Prince, on the 8th of October.

After the imposing ceremonies which necessarily attended the imperial coronation, the people, not forgetful of Him who had guided them through this arduous struggle in defence of those rights with which He had originally endowed them, marched to the church, where a Te Deum was sung to commemorate the important transactions of this memorable day. From this place of solemnity the whole procession returned in the order in which they came to the government house; after which a grand illumination took place in all parts of the city, amid the roaring of cannon and every demonstration of joy that both language and action could possibly express.

In tracing the narrative of this remarkable revolution, we have purposely omitted the invasion of the British from 1793 to 1798. Suffice it to say, that after a profuse waste of blood and treasure during five years, Great Britain was constrained to withdraw the remnant of her troops, acknowledge the independence of the island as a neutral power, and relinquish forever all pretensions to Hayti.

Such, then, is a brief outline of the principal features in the history of this new-born empire, as recorded by Edwards, Rainsford, and Coke, and as given me from the lips of veterans yet upon the soil. The principal changes since are briefly these:

The reign of the emperor Dessalines was short and turbulent, and his designs against the mulattoes cost him his life. After the death of Dessalines, (in 1807,) General Christophe was made chief magistrate, and in 1811 he crowned himself King Henri I. Meanwhile the mulattoes having cause to distrust him also, elected General Petion, a companion of Rigaud, to preside in the south-west, which he did with great leniency and to the entire satisfaction of his constituents, by many of whom he is still affectionately remembered. He died in 1818. Christophe shot himself in 1820. In 1822, Boyer, who had been elected President, united the whole island under his government.

And this brings the chain of events up to those mentioned in our review of the history of the Spanish part of the island, to which the reader can refer for a statement of the principal changes from that time to the present.

Under President Geffrard the country is highly prosperous, such confidence being placed in the government that its paper currency is preferred by the people to silver coin.

Under Protestant influences, also, several large schools, in which hundreds of young girls and boys are being educated, promise in due time to present to the world a virtuous female offspring of these heroic revolutionists, adorned by all the graces attending the use of both the French and English languages, and a body of youths skilled at once in commerce, and in the sciences of government, the sword, the anvil, and the plow.

The president desires the immigration hither of young men and ladies who are capable of teaching French, "and also to undertake," he says, "the courses of our lyceums. In this case they would find employment immediately."

It is difficult to believe these fields of natural beauty, embellished with all the decorations of art, have at any time presented to earth and heaven such spectacles of horror as to cause even Europe, accustomed as it is to blood and fire, to stand aghast, and which will serve Americans as a finger-board of terror so long as slavery there exists. The torch of conflagration and the sword of destruction have marched in fearful union through the land, and covered the hills and plains with desolation. Tyranny, scorn, and retaliating vengeance have displayed their utmost rage, and in the end have given birth to an empire which has not only hurled its thunderbolts on its assailants, but at this moment bids defiance to the world.

In the days of imperial Rome it was the custom of Cicero and his haughty contemporaries to sneer at the wretchedness and barbarity of the Britons, just as Americans speak of Haytiens to-day; yet when we reflect how analogous the history of the seven-hilled city and that of the United States promises to be, that Hayti may yet become the counterpart of England, head-quarters of a colored American nationality, and supreme mistress of the Caribbean sea, she can well afford to leave

"Things of the future to fate."

LETTER XIV.

Grand Turk's and Caicos Islands.

AN ISLAND OF SALT—SIR EDWARD JORDAN, OF JAMAICA—HONOR TO THE BRITISH QUEEN—A STORY IN PARENTHESIS—THE POETRY OF SAILING.

> "Had ancient poets known this little spot—
> Poets who formed rich Edens in their thought—
> Arcadia's vales, Calypso's verdant bowers,
> Hesperia's groves, and Tempe's gayest flowers,
> Had ne'er appeared so beautiful and fair
> As these gay rocks and emerald islands are."

IT is usually no more to "dangle round" this sea than it is to cross Lake Erie. On this particular occasion, however, I very willingly reached these shores, for the little schooner Enterprise in which we had ventured was not much larger than a good-sized yawl—certainly not over six tons burthen. The waves inundated us at pleasure, wetting even the letters in my breast coat-pocket, filling our faces at times with its slashing foam, and drenching us thoroughly to the inmost thread. But our schooner skimmed along like a sea-gull, and within thirty-two hours we were once again on land, dry enough for all practical purposes.

Nice little schooner—the waves might as well have undertaken to drown a fish!

There is not a natural hill on all Turk's Island. The shores are but a few feet above the level of the sea, and the interior is scooped out like a basin. This basin is artificially subdivided into innumerable troughs or ponds, into which water is admitted by canals from the sea, whence it evaporates leaving beds of salt. This salt is then raked into hills, so that as you approach these shores you have the extraordinary sight of an island studded with salt-hills.

The slight elevation of the land also permits the wind to pass uninterruptedly over its limestone surface, which accounts for the even temperature and perfect health of the island. The thermometer fell to-day from 86° to 77° Fahrenheit, which is the hottest and the coldest they have had it this summer. But, as you will readily perceive, the absence of all barriers to the winds subjects the colony to the terrific ravages of every ocean storm that chooses to sweep this way. At this very moment the large and substantial mansion in which I am writing trembles like an aspen-leaf, and I am fearful that the few cocoa-nut trees and flower plants bending before the storm on every side will be speedily swept away. Heaven spare the verdure!—the people can look out for themselves. Generally speaking, the winds are soft as a sigh. The gale ebbs to a gentle zephyr; the cloud passes on to Mobile, or wherever else it is bound, leaving these islands gayer for its shower; the huge West Indian sun, apparently magnified to six times its usual diameter, sinks into the crimsoned sea; the heavenly twilight comes on once more, and earth, sea, and sky are all once again tranquilly imparadised. The effect of these transitions on the mind is imperative. The most commonplace, matter-of-fact personage you have in America can not spend a summer around these islands and amid these scenes without having transitory poetic visions flash through his inmost being. But do not think I intend to dwell any further on these Elysian things. If you have a correspondent capable of describing them, send him along. A keen sense of my inability to do so constrains me to desist as from an attempt to comprehend the Infinite.

According to the theory of certain American statesmen, Turk's Island properly belongs to Hayti; at least, it is on the borders of the Haytien sea, and and is as much beholden to Hayti for its support as Cuba is to the United States. As luck has it, however, Turk's Island really belongs to the British, and Cuba, it would seem,

"By some o'r hasty angel was misplaced."

These, then, are a group of the celebrated British West Indies, and form a part of the governmental jurisdiction of Jamaica. It is with rare pleasure that I mention the latter fact, (since "next to being great one's self it is desirable to have a true relish for greatness,") for it gives me an opportunity to inform you that the order of knighthood has recently been conferred by Her Britannic Majesty on Sir Edward Jordan, Mayor of the city of Kingston and Prime Minister of Jamaica—a degree of dignity never before attained by a colored man, as I believe, since the British government began. The day of the Anglo-African in America has not yet clearly dawned, but it is dawning. A great many of the officers here, too, are colored. How strange it seems to stand before a large, fine-looking black or colored man, entitled Sir, Honorable, Esquire, and the like! To save me, I cannot realize it, although I see, hear, and shake hands with them every day.

But the grand source of interest to you and to me is, of course, the slaves manumitted by the magnanimity of the British government some twenty-six years agone. It is strangely interesting to hear them tell of parties making their escape to Hayti by sail-boats previous to the act of emancipation, sometimes sailing swift and direct, and at others dodging under the lee of the Caicos reefs until pursuit had been suspended, reminding one much of our Canadian friends. The history of the escape of slaves in our day is as full of heroism as any history in the world.

The neatness and cleanly appearance of the masses are actually surprising. I say it with all due respect, but, take them all in all, the colored people really present a better appearance than the whites. The latter, however, for reasons which you will already have anticipated, are of course more wealthy and intelligent—for which reason, also, they have heretofore been entirely at the head of political affairs. It is only recently that the blacks, who are in the majority, began to tread on their political heels. Some of the whites do not like to see this, but the easiest way for them is to allow themselves to be peacefully absorbed by the colored race in these regions, for their destiny is sealed.

The Caicos Islands, like most of the Bahamas, are but a series of coral reefs, more extensive in territory and less sterile than this portion of the colony; but their principal products are about the same—salt and shipwrecks. They are at once "the residence and the empire of danger." An American captain is now here selling the wreck of a cargo lately shipped from Boston to New Orleans—(Captain Elliot, ship Nauset, total wreck on North Caicos reef, July 7, 1860.) The population of the group inclusive is about five thousand, principally colored, who are remarkably industrious, if one is to judge from the rapidity with which they load a vessel with salt; and the essentially limited resources of the island would seem to admit of their being equally virtuous. Churches abound, and schooling may be had at the rate of three cents per week. Every thing is due to the English missionary societies for the healthy tone of morality and religion which prevails in these islands, and I must say, as I believe, chiefly to the Baptists.

But the great characteristic and most amusing peculiarity of these people is their inordinate attachment to the British crown. A captain of a schooner on the coast (black, but thoroughly British) one day overheard some reckless fellow speak disrespectfully of Queen Victoria. About every thing he thought of or said during the rest of the voyage was, "He insult my Queen," repeating "He insult my Queen" over and over again. They seem to regard Queen Victoria with about the same reverence that the Spanish Catholics bestow upon the Virgin Mary. Nor do I blame them for this, since, if England were crippled to-day, it would be difficult to say what would become of the world's humanity. It would be like extinguishing the sun!

Every thing is salty. You stand a chance to get some Boston ice here, which is a *rara avis* in this direction; but before you can get it congealed into cream you are bound to get salt into it, it would seem. A nice saloon, a good hotel, three churches, (English, Wesleyan, and Baptist,) and a first class Masonic lodge—at the head of which is a colored Esquire—together with its excessive salt propensities, are about the best things that can be said for Grand Turk's Island. Stay! I forget the "Royal Standard," a weekly journal, to the editor of which I am under obligations, and from which I clip the following

NOTICE.

On the first of August, the "Friendly Society" and the "Benevolent Union Society" of Salt Cay will march in procession from the Society Hall, at

11 o'clock A. M., to the Baptist chapel, where a sermon will be preached by the Rev. W. K. Rycoft on the occasion. By order, etc.,

JOHN L. WILLIAMS.

So much for the land of salt, and a farewell to its happy people, the most that can be said of whom is that they worship Queen Victoria.

(Let me tell you a story. In passing around these islands, we are one day with the Spanish, next day with the English, and the third with the French. It is sometimes diverting. I was sitting one warm afternoon before the door of a country-house, having a large green sward-yard sloping away to the road. The house was full of children, some of whom were, or pretended to be, studying their books. Well, suddenly there came pouring down a splendid summer shower, when, without a word, half a dozen of these little rogues, of both sexes, dropped their books, stripped off to the skin, and away they went sailing around the yard like so many water nymphs! In five minutes more they were all dressed, sitting down with their books, and looking as demure as if nothing had happened. "So there hadn't," except that one plump little girl *fell heels over head!* That is one way of taking a shower bath I never thought of.)

By the way, an American captain was this day looking at a number of hands, male and female, engaged in loading a vessel with salt. The women were employed holding the sacks, and tying them when filled.

"That's a smart gal," said the Yankee captain, pointing to an ebon Venus who was singing, dancing, and tossing the sacks around as merrily as your city girls ever " pawed" the piano.

A sleek-faced gentleman turned up his eyes at us, and inquired: "You lub dis gal, Cap'en ?"

"Thunder, no!" said the astonished American; "I don't love anybody!" Which remark, I guess, was not very far from the truth.

The vessel which I am now on board of is a full-rigged, finely-finished English brig. Her sails are all set, the wind blows fresh, and she cuts the water like a sword-fish. The captain cleared $1,400 on his trip out, with a cargo of lumber from the States. How much will our friend Wm. Whipper make in a year running his craft up a Canadian creek ? The tenacity with which our leading colored men embrace that short-sighted policy which teaches them to confine their enterprises to certain proscribed, prejudice-cursed districts, is not only extraordinary—it is marvellous.

The heavenly night comes on. The clouds in the sky look like ships on fire. The rising moon trembles upon the silver-sheeted waves in the east, while the receding sun burnishes the west, tinging the waters even to our very spray. And thus, in this sea of glory, do we skim along. *This* is the "poetry of sailing."

> "Thou glorious, shining, billowy sea,
> With ecstasy I gaze on thee!
> And as I gaze, thy billowy roll
> Wakes the deep feelings of my soul."

LETTER XV.

British Honduras.

THE ISLAND OF RUATAN—THE SAILOR'S LOVE STORY—THE SOVEREIGNTY OF THE BAY ISLANDS—ENGLISH VS. AMERICAN VIEW OF CENTRAL AMERICAN AFFAIRS.

Off Ruatan the New "Gibralter," Flower of the Bay Islands, and " Key to Spanish America."

IT certainly takes the impatience out of one to travel very much on a sail vessel. The dead certainty of your getting becalmed annihilates even contrary anticipation. But instead of murmuring at the irksome roll of this spell-bound ship, which flaps its sails as vainly as a bird with cropped wings, I, with genuine Spartan philosophy, will make the most of it by going visiting, that is, from the cabin to the forecastle. Here I take a seat beside an American; (for, my dear H., nobody ever knows what true friendship is until they have been shipwrecked, nor does any one conceive how mutual are the sympathies of persons coming from the same country, however remote their positions may have been, until they have met away from home.

and been surrounded by foreign influences. Strange as it may seem, I have not met a colored American out this way but who actually celebrates the Fourth of July.)

Instead of complaining of this ghastly calm, as I was about to say, I take a seat beside my friend Mr. Johnson, formerly of Plymouth, Massachusetts, from whom I learned the following important story, albeit, a love story. Important because it shows the correctness of that theory which assumes this,— the infusion of Northern blood as one of the means by which the more sluggish race of the tropics is to be quickened and given energy, and also how these seductive southern zones induce persons to sacrifice kindred, friends, and home, in order to live and die under their soothing influences.

The story is this: Some years ago he had sailed from Boston to Balize with a cargo of ice; was taken sick, and the captain of his vessel, having made all possible arrangements for his comfort, left him in the hospital to recover. He did so, and was just on the eve of going over to Jamaica to get on board a vessel in which to return home, when up stepped an elderly man, who accosted him in English and also in Yankee, to wit: "Guess you are from the States?" to which Mr. Johnson replied, of course, "You, too, I suppose?" The fact is, if you could not tell an American away from home by his looks, his salutatory phrases are as certain as an oddfellow's password.

So Mr. Dickinson, the elderly gentleman, was from the States also, and nothing would do but Mr. Johnson must accompany him to his home in Ruatan, there to spend a few weeks for old acquaintance' sake, and meanwhile strengthen his health. He went; but Mr. Johnson coming from the States had never seen so lovely an island, and certainly none so prolific as Ruatan. He found oranges selling for one dollar per barrel, and cocoa-nuts at a cent apiece; and that after being rowed a distance of six miles. He found also that good milch cows could be bought for six dollars each; and that upon one of the neighboring islands wild cattle were to be had for the sport of catching. On Utille, another island, also, almost in sight of Ruatan, is a settlement of whites, which, though small, is in a very flourishing condition; both being tributary to Ruatan. Altogether, he liked the appearance of things exceedingly.

Mr. Johnson not being one of your lazy visitors, soon began to make himself useful by assisting his friend Mr. Dickinson in whatever he might have to do; and so one day, with pants rolled up to his knees, he went over to a neighbor's to borrow some bags. This neighbor had a pretty niece who lived in Nicaragua, which is just over the way, and who was now on a visit to her uncle.

It was near dusk; his neighbor was not at home; but, with that careless indifference which travellers in the tropics will appreciate, he walked into the shanty, slightly nodded to some one he saw sitting in the corner, and immediately stretched himself out in a hammock.

The timid girl, less frightened at this rude freedom than at the bushy whiskers of the Northerner, answered his inquiries as to when her uncle would be in, curtsied, and left the room; but in doing so she discovered about the trimmest ancle and the neatest pair of stockings Mr. Johnson had ever beheld. It fixed him. He could not sleep after that without dreaming of the pretty feet, and, of course, pretty owner.

Mr. Johnson found business with his neighbor very often. The divinity went over home; Mr. Johnson had business over there also; and with genuine American grit obtained the old man's consent, and actually returned with his daughter.

Soon after this Mr. Johnson received from the
7*

States the mournful intelligence of his father's death, and, like a dutiful son, immediately sailed for Plymouth to see his mother and sisters. His brother, equally anxious with his mother and friends to have him stop at home, offered him a situation as clerk in a lawyer's office. But, alas! those pretty feet! They had caused him to sacrifice his home; and although shipwrecked in the attempt, he is now back in Ruatan, with no expectation of ever meeting his Plymouth friends again during life. "I told them," said he, "she was not quite so white as some of them, but she's a darn sight better-hearted;" which is very probably a fact. Mr. Johnson affirmed, also, that he could not be induced to leave Ruatan for the income of the most princely merchant in Boston; but I make allowances for a man who has a young wife with pretty feet.

Ruatan, as you are aware, is the principal one of the celebrated Bay Islands, the sovereignty of which has been so long in dispute. Nor can I settle the question as to whether the British claim is just or not; I can only give it to you as I get it.

In the first place you must know there is what may be called *two Hondurases*. That is, the State of Honduras, and these Bay Islands with a portion of the Musquito coast, constituting British Honduras, of which Balize is the capital. This will relieve a great many blunders people have perpetually fallen into.

When or by whom Ruatan was originally settled is now unknown. It was discovered by the Spaniards, and was afterwards occupied as a military post, but subsequently abandoned. Soon after the Emancipation Act took effect in Jamaica and the other British isles, a number of these emancipated slaves settled here, and the settlement is now multiplied to the number of about three thousand.

It becoming necessary for them to have a government, they sent to Jamaica for a magistrate to act as governor, voting him a salary of three thousand dollars, and, being British subjects, of course looked to Great Britain for protection. And so Great Britain claims the right to protect them; and she does protect them.

It was off this island that the pirate Walker rendezvoused the present summer; and from what I have said respecting the immigration hither of a few white Americans, you will probably suppose there might be some advantage taken of these islanders; but do not think it. Mr. William Walker's recent experience at Truxillo will probably induce him to respect Ruatan.

Nevertheless, Ruatan is measurably affected, of course, by the prosperity of the main land, and if the future administration of the United States government is to be as weak and vacillating as the past has been, it is difficult to say what is to be the end of these invasions.

At present there is but little communication between this excellent island and the United States. Thanks to your unjust policy, (wide-spread infamy,) the natives can not be induced to look towards America, and so can not see the difference between the Northern and Southern States. This feeling has been heightened recently by the fact that a merchant, who dealt in fruits with certain parties in New Orleans, went over there on business. He was also a British magistrate, and took with him the necessary papers to certify that fact. Hardly had he reached the shore before he was arrested and taken to prison; and when he supposed to estop their procedure by showing that he was a British magistrate, the New Orleans constable replied: "If Queen Victoria were to come over here, and she were black, I'd put her in jail!"

I am asked to point out, as I go along, what could be done whereby persons could gain a competence? Any thing in the shape of work will gain a competence,—the trouble being, in all these countries, that a living is too easily gained. But fruits are the principal export. Could a vessel be run between this and Baltimore, or any other respectable port of the United States, it would pay beyond a peradventure. It would also furnish the means of getting here safe the fruits from wasting, for want of occasional vessels, and also supply news; which is an inconceivable desideratum.

Land is offered at a shilling an acre; import duty is but two per cent., and exports free; which, considering the English language prevails, give it a decided advantage as a place of settlement.

Ruatan is but thirty miles from Truxillo, Honduras, and one hundred and twenty from Balize; and these are the only ways of getting here from New York, at a cost of sixty dollars. For the want of such a vessel as I have intimated, crops of oranges and limes are frequently swept into the sea. The Pine-apples are large and of a superior quality. Walk out into the grounds early in the morning, take a Machette and strike one open, and nothing can give you an idea of their flavor except to imagine you are sipping the nectar of the gods.

In the interior of the island are cocoa-nut groves, and other marks of improvement, such as an old fortress hid away from the sea, which clearly prove the island to have been anciently inhabited; but, like many other interesting objects which the historian fails to comprehend, by whom, or when, is left entirely to the conception of the poets.

> "Gone are all the barons bold;
> Gone are all the knights and squires;
> Gone the abbot, stern and cold,
> And the brotherhood of friars."

ENGLISH vs. AMERICAN VIEW OF CENTRAL AMERICAN AFFAIRS.

It is but fair to say the Hon. E. G. Squier shows very clearly the forced nature of the English claims, and that Ruatan rightly belongs to Honduras. But then I should think Mr. Squier, or any other American, would blush to talk about British *proclivities to piracy.*

The following are the views of Mr. Trollope (English) on the most important of Central American affairs,* who probably also intends by them to give Mr. S. a rap on the knuckles.

"As I have before stated, there was, some few years since, a considerable passenger traffic through Central America by the route of the lake of

---

* Anthony Trollope's West Indies and Spanish Main. Harper and Brothers.

Nicaragua. This of course was in the hands of the Americans, and the passengers were chiefly those going and coming between the Eastern States and California. They came down to Greytown at the mouth of the San Juan river, in steamers from New York, and, I believe, from various American ports, went up the San Juan river in other steamers, with flat bottoms, prepared for those waters, across the lake in the same way, and then by a good road over the intervening neck of land between the lake and the Pacific.

"Of course the Panama Railway has done much to interfere with this. In the first place, a rival route has thus been opened; though I doubt whether it would be a quicker route from New York to California if the way by the lake were well organized. And then, the company possessing the line of steamers running to Aspinwall from New York has been able to buy off the line which would otherwise run to Greytown.

"But this rivalship has not been the main cause of the total stoppage of the Nicaraguan route. The filibusters came into that land and destroyed every thing. They dropped down from California, or Realego, Leon, Managua, and all the western coast of Nicaragua. Then others came from the

South-eastern States, from Mobile, and New Orleans, and swarmed up the river San Juan, devouring every thing before them.

"There can be no doubt that Walker's idea, in his attempt to possess himself of this country, was, that he should become master of the passage across the Isthmus. He saw, as so many others have seen, the importance of the locality in this point of view; and he probably felt that if he could make himself lord of the soil, by his own exertions and on his own bottom, his mother country, the United States, would not be slow to recognize him. 'I,' he would have said, 'have procured for you the ownership of the road which is so desirable for you. Pay me by making me your lieutenant here, and protecting me in that position.'

"The idea was not badly planned, but it was of course radically unjust. It was a contemplated filching of the road. And Walker found, as all men do find, that he could not get good tools to do bad work. He tried the job with a very rough lot of tools; and now, though he has done much harm to others, he has done very little good to himself. I do not think we shall hear much more of him.

"And among the worst injuries which he has done is this disturbance of the lake traffic. This route has been altogether abandoned. There, in the San Juan river, is to be seen one old steamer, with its bottom upwards, a relic of the filibusters and their destruction.

"All along the banks tales are told of their injustice and sufferings. How recklessly they robbed on their journey up the country, and how they returned to Greytown — those who did return, whose bones are not whitening the lake shores— wounded, maimed, and miserable.

"Along the route traders were beginning to establish themselves; men prepared to provide the travellers with food and drink, and the boats with fuel for their steam. An end for the present has been put to all this. The weak governments of the country have been able to afford no protection to these men, and, placed as they were beyond the protection of England or the United States, they have been completely open to attack. The filibusters for a while have destroyed the transit through Nicaragua; and it is hardly matter of surprise that the president of that land, the neighboring republic, should catch at any scheme which proposes to give them back this advantage, especially when promise is made of the additional advantage of effectual protection.

"To us Englishmen it is a matter of indifference in whose hands the transit may be, so long as it is free and open to the world; so long as a difference of nationality creates no difference in the fares charged, or in the facilities afforded. For our own purposes I have no doubt the Panama line is the best, and will be the route we shall use. But we should be delighted to see a second line opened. If Mr. Squier can accomplish his line through Honduras we shall give him great honor, and acknowledge that he has done the world a service. Meantime we shall be very happy to see the lake transit reëstablished."

There is no hope for the Central American States except by intervention on the part of some government capable of protecting them.

LETTER XVI.

Conclusive Summary.

CONCISE DESCRIPTION OF THE SPANISH MAIN — DOMINICANA REVIEWED — THE MAGNIFICENT BAY OF SAMANA — CONCLUSIVE SUMMARY.

THUS have I endeavored to seize on whatever might seem to be of importance, and at the same time interesting to such of your readers as desired to have some more general information respecting tropical America.

I am aware that I have not analyzed the soil, nor (so long as it produced well) have I cared whether it was "composed of the *débris* of these limestones and lava mountains," or "tempered by the decaying vegetation of the centuries past." Nor have I entered into any essay to show how the lofty sierras of Honduras differed from those of Nicaragua, or those of the islands from the Spanish Main. It would be easy to give you a chapter stating that "the summits of some of them are of hard sandstone or granite; some are covered with layers of mould of different colors and density, sometimes mixed with stones of different degrees of hardness, and more or less calcinable; and some of them of various vitrifiable substances." But I take it that the way to make a thing useful is also to have it agreeable. Who reads, for example, Mr. Wells' well-written but ponderous " Travels and Explorations in Honduras " ?

Central America, by common assent, not only realizes in its geographical position the ancient idea of the centre of the world, but is in its physical aspect and configuration of surface an epitome of all the countries and of all climes. "High mountain ranges, isolated peaks, elevated table lands, and broad and fertile plains, are here grouped together, relieved by beautiful lakes and majestic rivers; the whole teeming with animal and vegetable life, and possessing every variety of climate from torrid heat to the cool and bracing temperature of eternal spring."

On the Atlantic slope rain falls in greater or less abundance for the entire year; vegetation is rank, and the climate damp and proportionately insalubrious, while the Pacific slope and the elevated regions of the interior are comparatively dry and healthy.

With this variety of "physical circumstances," also, the people differ, and have always differed, in a direct and corresponding ratio; the inhabitants of the cool and healthy regions having at the time of the discovery systematized forms of government and worship, while the hotter and less salubrious coasts were occupied by a distinct family of men unfixed in their abodes, having no social enjoyments, and living on the natural fruits of the earth. In Central America, therefore, Dr. Smith's celebrated essay on "Civilization—its Independence of Physical Circumstance," receives a striking illustration, the damp Musquito coasts having propagated only a rude tribe of men; while San Salvador, for example, sustains a population highly civilized, and equal in number to New England.

But I have dwelt at most length on the island of Hayti, because it is a source of greatest interest to us, and because there is perhaps no country the intrinsic value of which is so little known; and while I can see no objection but every thing to encourage by governmental influence the establishment of a colony in some parts of the Central American States, neither do I know why it might not be established in the Spanish territory of Hayti. I have given another gentleman's views, which are worth more than my own, as to the vast population the country is capable of sustaining, and have shown that especially from Porto Cabello west, to the Bay of Samana east, no finer province could certainly be desired. That noble bay, as I am informed, has been surveyed heretofore by a corps of American engineers, who pronounced it the choicest point for a naval station on the Caribbean coasts. It is also assumed, from the rapid increase of the coral reefs in the Bahama channels, that this in time will furnish the only safe channel for California steamers, and even for larger vessels bound from the Northern States to New Orleans. I have nothing to do with that, further than to state it as I have it. The insurance companies will however appreciate this assumption, if we are to judge from the number of wrecks which have recently occurred between the Caicos and Florida reefs.

Surrounding the bay of Samana are beds of coal as if on purpose to supply such steamers; but they now lie unworked, useless, and almost unknown. Into this bay empties the Yuna river, which takes its rise far back in the northern and middle range of mountains, and, fed by innumerable tributaries, winds its course towards this magnificent harbor through the widest portion of the Royal plains.

"In briefly describing the principal bays of

Dominicana," says Mr. Courtney, "the first of importance is the far-famed and magnificent bay of Samana, at the north-eastern end of the island, at the mouth of the Yuna river. It is about fifty miles from east to west, and varying in width from fifteen to twenty miles, and of a great depth. The entrance to it is at the east end, and is about a mile wide, as beyond that is shoal water, to the south side some little islands and bars appearing above the surface. An old fort, erected long since on the high bluff on the north side, a few miles above the mouth and before it widens out, commands its entrance. The hills and mountains on either side of the bay rise back from it to a great height, their sides being covered with beautiful slopes, plateaus, and benches. The coasts are here and there indented with minor bays and inlets, the most important of which is at the town of Samana, about twenty-five miles up the bay on the north side. It is a land-locked harbor and very deep, as are all the inlets. The view of the bay from either side across to the opposite shores, covered as it is with swarms of ducks and swans and other water fowl; and the coasts and hills and mountains covered with flowers and verdure and fruit, is truly beautiful and sublime, equalling, if not surpassing, in beauty and magnificence, the Bay of Naples, and is obviously the key to the Gulf of Mexico.

"Here all the navies of the world could lie at anchor in safety."

It would be useless for me to give a minute description of each particular bay in each particular State, thus swelling these pages into the usual ponderous three-dollar volumes which nobody buys, and so none read. I am aware that the Bay of Fonseca, and others on the Spanish Main, are equally deserving, if necessary, to be described. Mr. Wells has shown this, and also that the interior districts of Honduras are as rich in silver and gold as any region of which California can boast. I understand, however, that parties have since been formed on the strength of Mr. Wells' report, and thoroughly equipped for mining operations. But as I am informed, they were not allowed to enter the interior in consequence of those filibustering propensities which all white Americans are supposed to possess.

A party organized to work the mines on a small scale in Dominicana has lately sailed for the island. They will not be interrupted by the present government, but the durability of that government is, I am sorry to say, a question which may be agitated, and even settled, *before I finish writing this book*.

And now I have struck the key note of all I have to say. The most beautiful countries in the world are the most lamentably ill-governed. It makes no difference to any one having foreign protection, as to their personal safety, whether there be revolution or not. This white Americans and all Englishmen or anybody else have, but the free colored people of America. They have no protection anywhere.

Now this is a shame and a disgrace to the civilized world. But so it is, and, as Mr. Douglas would ask, "What are you going to do about it?"

I have no reason to doubt the sincerity of such eminent persons as have proposed to acknowledge the independence of these governments, form treaties therewith, and even to purchase territory and provide the means whereby a settlement could be established. I have rather much cause to believe the new government (that is to be) will give the subject earnest consideration. Nothing could be more just, and, as I believe, wise or popular. I know that such a measure would not be opposed by the people of the tropics, for there are many who entertain progressive ideas, and who have sympathies in common with Americans, who, the moment a protected settlement were established, would flock thither from the neighboring States and islands, and immediately swell the number of the original emigrants. I say I know this, because so many have said so, among whom could be mentioned English and American families, white and colored. But it pains me to say, the truth is, unless this protection could be given, or unless a sufficient number could emigrate (which they are not able to do) to protect themselves, none of these States seem to be in a sufficiently reliable condition to prevent such a movement from being a matter of great risk.

I have shown, I think, which was the object of this visit, what might be accomplished provided the government should provide means, never so small, towards the furtherance of such a movement.

It is the only way by which a colony to any extent could be permanently established, which would give tone and stability to the government there, and turn the important commerce of the tropics in this direction. There are now probably ten European vessels in the harbor of Spanish America, but especially of Dominicana, where there is one belonging to the United States, although the latter is the natural market, from which they receive entirely their flour and salted pork. (Merchants of Cincinnati will appreciate this.)

I presume it would be difficult to find an American merchant in any of the Spanish States, who had not succeeded in making a fortune by the great advantages of trade in mahogany, dye-woods, hides, and tobacco, almost immediately after commencing business, but who has not as invariably lost it, in whole or in part, by the depression of currency in consequence of the momentary revolutions.

How grandly would both these and *those* States "loom up in the eyes of the world," if, abandoning that policy which makes them the indiscriminate oppressors of the weak, the American people should set themselves at work through their new administration, to secure by this means the commerce of those countries; give them peace, and forever wipe out the stain which Walker has cast upon the very name of all who boast themselves citizens of this republic. Such a measure would in some degree recompense the colored race for the services they have rendered to the government, the fruits of which they have not been permitted to enjoy; would make this great nation less obnoxious to the weak;

lay the foundation of a future empire; and cause those lovely regions to bloom with industry and skill as they now bloom with eternal verdure.

END.

APPENDIX.

(FROM THE ANGLO-AFRICAN MAGAZINE.)

The Anglo-African Empire.

"Do these things mean nothing? What the tender and poetic youth dreams to-day and conjures up with inarticulate speech, is to-morrow the vociferated result of public opinion, and the day after is the charter of nations."—*Phillips*.

THE stars of the tropics are the guiding stars of the age. The sympathy of the world is with the South, and the tendencies of things are southward. The controlling influence of the great commercial staple of our Southern States, the growing demand for the productions of the tropics, the discovery of gold toward the torrid zone, and a consequent want of labor in that direction, indicate firmly the force of these assertions. Other causes, apparently indirect or yet apparently opposed, such as the disappearance of slavery from Maine to Maryland, and the rapidity with which the slaves are hurried further south, might be cited on the one hand; and on the other the filibustering propensities of Southern fire-eaters as the unerring and immutable laws of destiny, guided by an all-wise and overruling Providence. "The coral zoöphite does not know that while it builds itself a house it also creates an island for the world;" and the master, as he pays the passage of his slave from the more Northern slave States to New Mexico, is but the rude agent of a superior power, urging him to more inviting fields for enterprise, and for his higher and more responsible duties as a freeman.

Reforms do not go backwards, nor filibustering northwards, and " nothing is more certain than that the slaves are to be free;" but the problem as to what position they are to sustain as freemen is but little thought of, and, of course, less understood. It is true some suggestions have been offered on this subject, foremost among which stands that of Mr. Helper, as the most absurd and ridiculous. It did not occur to Mr. Helper, when he suggested the broad idea of chartering all the vessels lying around loose for the huddling together of the blacks after emancipation and shipping them off to Africa, —it did not occur to him that they were men, and might not wish to go; at least it did not occur to him that they were *men*. So I make the suggestion for his benefit, and for the benefit of those who may come after him, this being a question not to be settled by arbitrary means, but by means which shall meet the approbation of all parties concerned, nor yet forgetting that at the head of these parties stands Him whose name is not to be mentioned without reverence.

Whence comes the colored people's instinctive horror of colonization in Africa? Colonizationists say they can not account for it, since Africa is their fatherland. But if this were any argument, I could account for it by the simple affirmation that it is not their fatherland. The truth is, "Time has shown that the causes which have produced races never to improve Africa, but to abandon it, and give their vigor and derive their strength from other climes, is not to be reversed by the best efforts of the best men." Besides this, charity begins at home. Allowing that the colonizationists, by sending a few handfuls of colored men to Africa, may plant the germ of civilization there, that the seed may spread or the fire may flame until the whole continent becomes illuminated with Christian love, and her sons stand forth regenerated and redeemed from the dark superstition that enthralled them. Then what?

It is a great deal, and a great deal more than we can hope for, and a hero is he who will sacrifice his life in making the attempt to bring about such a magnificent result; but in doing this very little will be accomplished for the millions who remain, increasing, on this continent.

Nevertheless, there is a growing disposition among colored men of thought to abandon that policy which teaches them to cling to the skirts of the white people for support, and to emigrate to Africa, Hayti, or wherever else they may expect to better their condition; and it is encouraging to know that the time is at hand when men can speak their convictions on this subject without being made the victims of iliterate abuse and indiscriminate denunciation, all of which is the natural result of more general information, and which will lead to the discovery at last of what is to be the final purpose of American slavery—the destiny of the colored race after slavery shall be abolished.

The history of Hayti and Jamaica, and of the American tropics generally, indicates the propagation of the colored race, exclusive of whites or blacks. (This is simply calling things by their right names, for which the compiler of these facts expects to be made the most popular writer of the age, of being highly flattered, infinitely abused, feared, hated, and all that attends the discovery of truth generally.) Throughout the West Indies, with the single exception of Cuba, the whites have been unable to keep up their numbers, and in that instance only by a recent flood of immigration on a large scale from Europe. The colored race, on the contrary, is perfectly well adapted to this region, and luxuriates in it; and it is only through their agency that some small portion of the torrid zone has been brought within the circle of civilized industry. I have said their history would prove this.

When discovered by the Spaniards these islands were inhabited by a colored people not unlike our Indians. Their homes were invaded; they were reduced to a state of miserable vassalage, and the proud Caucasian stalked about, the conqueror of every spot of earth his avarice or cupidity desired. The natives, unable to endure the persecutions to which they were subjected, withered and fell like the autumn leaves, and Africa became the hunting-ground of the slave pirate for hardier and more enduring slaves.

Africa became their hunting-ground, and quiet villagers were startled in the dead of night to behold their huts in flames, and to hear the shrieks of their fellow-men and fellow-women, who were being torn away from their native homes as victims for the slave-ship, there to suffer all the tortures of the yoke and the branding-iron, and finally to be landed, if at all, on the American coast, with no other prospect than that of a life-bondage spread out before them. This state of wickedness continued, so far as England was concerned, until its glaring outrages challenged the attention of the British realm, and until the Parliament of England passed an act declaring all British subjects should be free;—"An act of legislation which, for justice and magnanimity, stands unrivalled in the annals of the world, and which will be the glory of England and the admiration of posterity when her proudest military and naval achievements shall have faded from the recollection of mankind;" an act of legislation which restored the liberties of eight hundred thousand of our fellow-men, *and left them in possession of superior claims and circumstances to those from which they had been originally removed,* (because, undoubtedly, the chances of any free man are better upon this continent than in Africa.)

Then came a series of American slanders: "Jamaica was ruined;" "the negro unfit for freedom;" and the downfall of prosperity and the loss of trade were everywhere said to be inevitable.

But the negro and his descendants are proof against slander and against the New York Herald, which terms are soon to be synonymous. Jamaica was not ruined: but, while these complaints were raised against her population, 40,000 land patents, varying from ten to one hundred acres each, were being taken up in a single year! Lands having been provided and schools introduced, happiness began to smile, prosperity reäppeared, and the whole country was redeemed from what had been a field of terror to what promises to become the very garden of the Western world.

This is said to be an axiom of political philosophy upon which it is safe to rely: *For any people to maintain their rights, they must constitute an essential part of the ruling element of the country in which they live.* The whites of the tropics are but few in number. They have heretofore sustained themselves by their superior wealth and intelligence. But, as fast as the colored people rise in this respect, their white rulers are pushed aside to make way for officers of their own race. This is perfectly natural. When a colony of Norwegians come over from Norway and settle a county in Wisconsin, do they elect a yankee to represent them? Norwegians elect Norwegians, Germans elect Germans, and colored men elect colored men, whenever they have the opportunity.

Even now a large majority of the subordinate officers of Jamaica, I understand, are colored men. The Parliament is about equally divided, and the Attorney-General and Emigration Agent-General are colored men; and it is fair to assume, within a few years of the date of this paper, there will not be a single white man throughout the West Indies occupying a position within the gift of the people.

A retired merchant of Philadelphia, a man of large thought and liberal views, having an experience of fifteen or twenty years' residence in Hayti, in reply to certain letters asking for information and advice respecting the subject now under consideration, published a pamphlet in which he says: "There is a long view as well as a short view to be taken of every great question which bears upon human progress; but we are often unable or unwilling to take the former, until some time after a question is settled.

"'Manifest destiny' has been, for some years, a familiar and accepted phrase in the mouths of our politicians, and each class suggests a plan for carrying it out in accordance with its own specific interests, or some preconceived theory. The pro-slavery adventurer may yet gain a footing in Central America, but it will not be to establish slavery. Slavery once abolished, has never been reëstablished in the same place, in America, except in one instance—that of the smaller French colonies, now again free. The vain effort to reënslave St. Domingo cost the French forty thousand men. The free negro, that nothing else can arouse, will fight against the replacement of the yoke which he has once thrown off; and the number of these in Central America is sufficient to prove a stumbling-block if not a barrier to its return. To reëstablish slavery permanently, where it is has once been abolished, is to swim against the great moral current of the age.

"We can acknowledge to-day that the persecution of the Puritans by Laud and his predecessors, only intended, as it was, to produce conformity to the Church, really produced New England. And we can now see that the obstinacy of George the Third was as much a cause of the Declaration of Independence, at the time it was made, as the perseverance of John Adams,—the one being the necessary counterpart of the other, the two together forming the entire implement which clipped the tie. Now if we can make the above admissions in respect to these, the two greatest settled questions of modern times, without excusing either persecution or obstinacy in wrong, but keeping steadily in view that every man is responsible for the motives which govern his conduct, be the result of that conduct what it may, why should we not begin to look at this, the third great question of the same class, still *unsettled*, from the same point of view?

"*If, then, I were asked what was probably the final purpose of negro slavery, I should answer—To furnish the basis of a free population for the tropics of America.*

"I believe that the Anglo-Americans, with the Africans, whom a part of the former now hold in bondage, will one day unite to form this race for the tropics, with or without combination with the races already there. But whether the African quota of it shall be transferred thither by convulsive or organized movements—or be gradually thinned out from their present abode, as from a great nursery, by directed but spontaneous transition—or retire, by degrees, with the 'poor whites,' before the peaceful encroachments of robust Northern labor, it would be useless now to conjecture. It is enough now to know that labor, like capital, goes in the end to the place where it is most wanted: and that labor, free from the destructive element of caste, has been, and still is, the great desideratum of the tropics, as it is of all other places which do not already possess it. I have already spoken of the presumed ability of the Southern States to spare this kind of labor. Should there, however, prove to be any part of the Union where the climate or the culture really requires the labor of the black man, then there he will remain, and eventually be absorbed by the dominant race; and from that point the complexion of our population will begin to shade off into that of the dark belt of Anglo-Africans, which will then extend across the northern tropics.

"I know that most of our Northern people, while they demand, in the strongest terms, all the rights of man for the negro or mulatto, are unable to eradicate from their minds a deeply-grounded prejudice against his person. In spite of themselves, they shrink from the thought of an amalgamation such as the foregoing observations imply. But these friends are not aware how quickly this prejudice begins to melt away as soon as one has entered any part of the tropics where the African race is in the ascendant, or where people of colored blood have attained to such social consideration as to make themselves respected. I suppose no Northern man ever forgets the occasion when, for the first time, he arrives at such a place, and the colored merchant to whom he is addressed comes forward, with the self-possession which attends self-respect, and offers him his hand. He begins to be healed of his prejudice from that hour."

I am also aware that the notion prevails generally in the United States that the mulatto has no vitality of race; that after three or four generations he dies out. This idea, I believe, finds its strongest advocates among the slaveholders and the readers of De Bow's "Review," and possibly it may be correct when applied to the colder latitudes; but I have no reason to think it is so in or near the tropics. Moreau de St. Mery, in his minute "Description of the French part of St. Domingo," says, with respect to the vitality of the mulatto, which term includes all persons of color, however slight, of mixed European and African descent: "Of all the combinations of white and black, the mulatto unites the most physical advantages. It is he who derives the strongest constitution from these crossings of race, and who is the best suited to the climate of St. Domingo. To the strength and soberness of the negro he adds the grace of form and intelligence of the whites, and of all the human beings of St. Domingo he is the longest lived. . . I have already said they are well made and very intelligent; but they are as much given to idleness and love of repose as the negro.

Hermann Burmeister, Professor of Zoölogy in the University of Halle, who spent fourteen months, in 1850-51, in studying at Brazil the "Comparative Anatomy and Physiology of the American Negro," speaks thus of the Brazilian mulatto: "The greatest number of the colored inhabitants of Brazil are of the negro and European races, called mulattoes. It may be asserted that the inferior classes of the free population are composed of such. If ever there should be a republic, such as exists in the United States of America, as it is the aim of a numerous party in Brazil to establish, the whole class of artisans would doubtless consist of a colored population. * * * Already in every village and town the mulattoes are in the ascendant, and the traveller comes in contact with more of them than of whites." There is nothing in these extracts, or in the essay from which they are taken, to indicate that the Brazilian mulatto is dying out. These are the observations of a patient investigator and man of science, and they have the more value, inasmuch as they were not set down to support any particular theory. The Professor speaks elsewhere in high but qualified terms of the moral and intellectual qualities of the mulatto, coming to conclusions similar to those of Moreau de St. Mery, except that he does not accuse them of indolence.

The author of "Remarks on Hayti and the Mulatto," whose experience as a merchant I have mentioned, further says:

"This race, if on the white side it derives its blood from either the English or French stock, possesses within itself a combination of all the mental and physical qualities necessary to form a civilized and progressive population for the tropics, *and it is the only race yet found of which this can be said.*"

"I have no desire to undervalue the blacks of Hayti. I have found many shrewd, worthy, and intelligent men among them; and the country, it is well known, has produced several black men of a high order of talent; but these have been exceptional cases, like the King Philips, Hendricks, Tecumsehs, and Red Jackets, of our North American Indians. As a race, they do not get on. *The same may be said of every other original race.* The blacks form no exception to the well-known law, that culture and advancement in man are the result of a combination of races."

continent with the whites, and the two empires being known respectively as Anglo-American and Anglo-African.

In conclusion, I desire to return my thanks for the complimentary manner in which the preceding communications have been received; and I would fain hope they might be as favorably regarded now that they are presented in this present form.

How proudly will the colored race honor that day, when, abandoning a policy which teaches them to cling to the skirts of the white people for support, they shall set themselves zealously at work to create a position of their own—an empire which shall challenge the admiration of the world, rivalling the glory of their historic ancestors, whose undying fame was chronicled by the everlasting pyramids at the dawn of civilization upon mankind.

> "Hope of the world! *the rising race*
> May heaven with fostering love embrace;
> And, turning to a whiter page,
> Commence with them *a better age;*
> An age of light and joy, which we,
> Alas! in prospect only see."

them, is by some scheme *which will meet the approbation of both—one which the parties themselves will execute."—Hon. Preston King.*

"Among all feasible things, there is nothing that in my judgment would so much promote a peaceful abolition of slavery as your son's plan."—*Hon. Gerrit Smith to F. P. Blair, Sen.*

"The feeling of the free blacks in relation to African colonization is no criterion by which to judge of the success of American intertropical emigration. . . . I am confident that with proper inducements to be held out before them in regard to security of liberty and property, and prospects for well-doing, I could muster two hundred emigrant families or about one thousand colored persons annually for the next five years, of the very best class for colonial settlement and industry, from various parts of the United States and Canada, who would gladly embark for homes in our American tropics."—*Rev. J. T. Holly.*

To the above might be added the views and opinions of many of the most eminent men in Ohio, Missouri, Illinois, Maryland, and other States, among them the Hon. Mr. Bates, and Sam'l T. Glover, Esq., of St. Louis. But none seem more appropriate to close this volume than the following from the Rev. Dr. Duffield, of Detroit.

Detroit, Feb. 18, 1860.

DEAR BRO. KENDALL:—

Allow me to commend to your attention the object in which Mr. Harris has embarked. I think very favorably of it on various grounds, but regard it as especially indicative of God's providential designs in relation to the introduction of the gospel into that portion of our American continent which

REMARKS.

I have no desire to retain, by the republishing of the above extracts, the appellation of "Defender of the Mulattoes;" but have inserted them here, that they may not be misunderstood. All I have to say is, that I believe it would be actually more proper, numerically speaking, to call at least the free persons of African descent in America, *colored* or mulattoes, rather than negroes. Yet, how often do we hear respectable men of all parties, talk of "Negro nationalities," and regarding the two races as "two negative poles mutually repelling each other," leaving no middle ground for the great mass of the colored people or mulattoes, whom, as some say, "God did not make." Instead of such impiety, and in place of sending one-half of the colored people to establish black nationalities in Africa, leaving the other half to be absorbed by the whites, I think it is much more liberal to regard them as one people, the political destiny of whom is unknown, or at best but begun to be discerned. To divide the colored people at this late day by any such process, would seem to me *like splitting a child in twain*, in order to give one half to its mother and the other to its father. *I go for a colored nationality*, that shall divide the

OPINIONS OF DISTINGUISHED STATESMEN AND PHILANTHROPISTS.

"My proposition is simply to provide for the peaceful emigration of all those free colored persons of African descent who may desire so to emigrate to some place in Central or South America. . . . I believe the time has ripened for the execution of the plan originated by Jefferson in his day, agreed in by Madison and Monroe and all the earlier and better statesmen of the Republic, both North and South.—*Speech of Senator Doolittle.*

"Instead, therefore, of being an expense to the nation, the foundation of such a colony would be the grandest commercial enterprise of the age. . . . .

"Are the young merchants of Boston and of America indifferent to an enterprise which would give to our commerce, without a rival, such an empire as that to which I have pointed?—an empire not to be won by cruelty and conquest, but by peaceful and benignant means, and by imparting to others the inestimable blessings of liberty which we enjoy, and removing from our midst the only cause which threatens the prosperity and stability of the Union . . ."—*Speech of Hon. F. P. Blair, Boston.*

"It is my intention to use every effort to give practical effect to the propositions submitted to Congress, and I believe that the colored people themselves can give very efficient aid in the matter. If they will only let it be known that they approve, and are themselves willing to act upon the proposition, it will give it a great impulse."—*Hon. F. P. Blair—Letter to J. D. Harris.*

"The only mode in which we can relieve our country, relieve the blacks and whites, and provide separate homes for has attracted our attention, and which led yourself with me to memorialize the General Assembly on the subject of commencing a system of missions in Mexico, Central and Southern America. I had intended writing to you on the subject with a view to the prosecution of the matter of our memorial next spring, when the Assembly meets at Pittsburg. I know not, nor can I learn, what has been done in pursuance of the action of the last General Assembly. The whole matter as reported I failed to understand, and have since had no light shed upon the subject. May not this movement prove an occasion, if not of connection to the mission, of bespeaking a deeper interest in behalf of our benighted populations of Central and Southern America than has yet been felt by and in our country. . . .

Truly Yours,

GEO. DUFFIELD.

REV. DR. KENDALL, of Pittsburg, Pa.

www.ingramcontent.com/pod-product-compliance
Lightning Source LLC
Chambersburg PA
CBHW032156160426
43197CB00008B/935